Holy Hell

PATRICIA FEENAN

FONTAINE
—PRESS—

Words, once published, have a life of their own.

Copyright © 2012 Patricia Feenan

Published by Fontaine Press
P.O. Box 948, Fremantle,
Western Australia 6959
www.fontainepress.com

ISBN: 978-0-9873565-4-3
A catalogue record for this book is available from the National Library of Australia.

For my devout Catholic parents, Mollie and Jack, who mercifully didn't ever learn of this terrible story but whose determination and fairness, passed on to their three daughters, enabled me to write about it.

Foreword

How would you react if told by a member of your family they had been sexually abused? Imagine your brother, sister or one of your own children coming to you for help. Then consider what you would do when you learn the perpetrator of those vile acts was one of your closest friends, respected, a person whom you trusted and had taken into the very midst of your family, your Parish Priest. How would you feel? Shocked, betrayed, self-blaming are all appropriate descriptions but most of all hurt, that terrible hurt that originates deep inside, surfacing only to overwhelm you.

Fortunately they are questions most of us will never have to face, we pray not anyway. Patricia Feenan however, did have to face those questions. She was exposed to all those emotions and more. As a good mum she was intent on raising her boys in a loving atmosphere surrounded by her extended and helpful family.

The Catholic Church was a big part of that family. The church wasn't just something they visited each Sunday; it was an intricate part of how they lived their lives. So when Father James Fletcher brought them into his close circle of friends they felt humbled and honoured, welcoming him as a regular visitor for meals, family celebrations and sharing his confidence. To learn this man violated and destroyed the childhood of Patricia's eldest son also destroyed her, irreparably damaging her faith in the church.

This book takes you on Patricia Feenan's personal journey. It is raw, revealing her inner-most emotions and thoughts as she lays open the wounds for you the reader, taking you from the mysterious behavioural changes in her son, the horrifying revelation followed by the police investigation and trial. She also explains the betrayal and abandonment by her beloved church.

The story will shock and confront as it takes you through every parent's worst nightmare. It is also a story of healing and hope for the future. Patricia Feenan wasn't just a good mum; she is an extraordinary woman who never gave up the struggle to rescue her family from the terrible abyss of despair created by a paedophile priest.

I suppose it is uncommon for a former detective who investigated the crime to introduce a book on the matter. If sharing her story helps others understand and comprehend the unimaginable then it will have achieved all that Patricia Feenan hoped. For that reason when asked to write this foreword I never hesitated.

Detective Chief Inspector Peter Fox

1

There was a knock on the door of our small room. All eyes swivelled towards the door as the Judge's Associate entered and announced, "the jury will now take a one-hour lunch break."

It was Monday the 6th of December 2004 and the people – all precious to me – had spent the previous two weeks sitting in East Maitland Courthouse during the Criminal Trial of Catholic priest, James Patrick Fletcher, who had been charged with the sexual abuse of my eldest son, Daniel, now aged twenty-eight years. At the time of the abuse he was just thirteen years old. My son's three brothers had stood shoulder to shoulder, protecting him, giving him strength and then willed the jury to find the priest guilty as charged.

Now we looked at one another and tried not to let the disappointment show. We had been sitting apprehensively since lunchtime on the previous Thursday when the jury retired to consider its verdict. I told myself that the longer a verdict took to be delivered must surely mean that the jury was really considering the whole picture. For us, the appalled family, close friends and supporters who had shared the most extraordinary emotions through the trial and whose indignation and anger, on learning of Daniel's trauma, was palpable, it meant another uneasy meal break was looming. Another lunch, more brittle conversation and a strong sense of unreality faced us, but this time it would be different.

At the lunch break the three boys scattered in various directions to seek a respite from this abnormal and painful situation. We made a quick call to Canberra to give an update to Dominic, the anxious son who had returned to work there after spending two weeks with us. A permeating numbness had crept over our family and supporters as the trial and deliberation unfolded.

Throughout the trial, family and friends had provided lunch and we welcomed the normality of eating a sandwich in the green room which had been allocated to our family but which was only five steps from the courtroom itself. We didn't arrange lunch after the jury retired as we hoped that a decision would be reached quickly and we could leave that building forever. Optimistic or naive?

Five women, including myself, drove down to the local café and tried to buy lunch. The café was busy and we could not order quickly. I asked myself whether the waitresses and cooks sensed our trauma. Surely it was unusual for groups of people to sweep in, order a quick meal, huddle in conversation, consult watches every few minutes and then rush out. I was very uneasy at the delay and kept watching the clock as our hour's meal break diminished and so asked if we could have our sandwiches wrapped to take with us. As the clock ticked the remainder of the lunchtime away, my friend Margaret rushed to get her truck to transport us back to the courthouse and we piled in clutching our wrapped lunches.

I felt strongly and strangely that something monumental was about to happen. Trust those instincts, Pat; I will never doubt my instincts again. As soon as we returned to our little room, and were about to unwrap our lunches, the sheriff appeared at the door and said that the jury was coming back in to the courtroom. No panic at that stage as this had happened a few times since the jury had retired at 11.00 am the Thursday before. Bernard, my youngest son, who hadn't left the Courthouse for lunch, rang Daniel and his next eldest brother, Luke, and told them the jury was coming back. He couldn't reach his father, John. My dear youngest son then put his arm round me and there it stayed as Detective Sergeant Peter Fox, the wonderful police officer who had managed the whole investigation and arrest of the priest, rushed down the hallway saying, "Pat, they have reached a verdict!" Then we panicked as we were missing some of the family, including the victim, my beloved son Daniel. The Crown Prosecutor hurried up the stairs and thankfully Daniel, his partner, Donna, and Luke arrived on the run.

We jostled into the courtroom. I was surrounded by a wall of believers. Supporters of the priest, James Fletcher, gathered as well and took front row seats. I wondered why. I couldn't speak and surely everyone present could hear my heart thundering. I was visually assaulted by the number of policemen, corrective service and sheriff's office personnel who then stood ringing the dock and courtroom in contrast to the two uniformed officers who had been present for the trial. I gulped, turned around and smiled at my beautiful eldest son, his partner and his next wonderful brother, Luke. I quickly touched Detective Fox's hand, and then held tightly to my dear youngest son who was sitting beside me. An old friend held me from the other side. We watched the jury file in and I searched their faces unsuccessfully for some indication of their decision. I realised that I had been waiting for this moment for a very, very long time.

2

Where did this story begin? Where does any story ever begin? Is it at the moment of birth when a lusty cry startles two emotional, triumphant and excited young people into the realisation that they are indeed parents? Or is it later when circumstances converge to change their lives forever?

A life enjoyed before the evilness of paedophilia changed it forever is satisfying to relate.

As a young married couple and indeed through our courtship, John and I had very much enjoyed our times with my elder sister, Christine, and her husband at their farm at Comboyne, a rural and picturesque area west of Taree. The family would gather and share holiday periods and weekends away in the idyllic setting of mountains, rainforest and pretty creeks. Cattle mustering, fencing and creek flats' cricket were the constants and we all developed as young adults, sharing long talks by the open fire about our childhoods, our hopes for the future and the meaning of life. Work hard, respect others, laugh often and live our Catholic faith always.... that was our mantra.

Having developed such an appreciation for the country life, John and I started to look at our options for the future. By this time, we had two little boys, Daniel and Luke, and we decided that a life in some kind of a rural setting would be good for them, as well as fulfilling our needs for that peace and tranquillity we had experienced with my sister, her husband and their little girls. John's career as an accountant was established and I worked part time as a teacher. We knew we were not skilled enough to make a viable living from the land.

We realised we could have the best of both worlds if we could find a little rural property close enough to Newcastle so John could commute to work. In late 1978, we were thrilled to be able to purchase twenty-five acres in a little hamlet about forty minutes from Newcastle. What excitement, what dreams we had, as our adventure began. Our friends doubted our sanity as we prepared to leave our lovely home in suburbia and embark on such a different life. They smiled uneasily and wished us well.

Those same friends stayed loyal and became regular visitors to our little country estate where they and their children enjoyed the relaxed lifestyle we had happily adopted. Scarcely a weekend would go by when we didn't have at least two car loads of friends, bikes, food and pyjamas (in case the day evolved into bath and an evening meal) arrive and unload excited children. Our own excited boys would dance around the visitors' cars, be kissed by the friends, usually the mothers, and then disappear with their mates to play. We never saw them until they had worked up a thirst and prodigious hunger.

Those children are adults now and when together, relive every cricket match, diving tournament both in the pool and on the football field, mud fight and campout. They all remember the ants' nest as being a definite highlight on a visit to the farm. It was located on the side of the track. We never, ever did get around to calling it a driveway. What fun could be had, and was had, pelting the nest and watching the ants jump. What delicious danger the boys experienced on that bend in the track! Dominic became a very fast runner and I believe the visits to the ants in his early years were the basis for developing that speed.

In such an environment, the boys had no trouble embracing life, love and laughter. We commented often that among our closest friends, we were overwhelmed with boys. Twenty-two boys to three girls was the tally on one of those special visiting Sundays. With so much backyard cricket played, it is no surprise that all four boys became very good at the game and many of the boys' weekends, when older, were taken up with morning and afternoon cricket on Saturdays and then representative cricket on Sundays. I could write a book on grass stains and cricket whites and I wish that was the only book that I felt the need to write.

Daniel, as the leader of this wonderful clan of boys, grew into a place where he knew he was loved, respected and successful. In primary school and indeed secondary school, he was a very popular school captain, a clever student and sportsman and was also blessed with remarkable looks. Even his teachers commented on his beautiful face. His brothers received many compliments as well and so I suppose we didn't even register any reaction when the local priest told us how handsome and angelic our eldest son was. The boys all remember our talks about inner beauty being more important than looks, beauty being in the eye of the beholder, and outer beauty fading. Character was what we were about!

It would be unrealistic to describe our life as perfect but we were very much rewarded by happy kids making happy times. There was rivalry, but about backyard cricket, and a healthy competitive streak in all my sons which caused minor squabbles, better academic results and endless discussions about endless topics. There was teasing too and a lot of hilarity about ripping one another off but no doubt they will all remember the truism that 'too much laughter ends in tears.'

3

I remember the appointment of Father James Fletcher to the Dungog Parish. We were a practising Catholic family and our faith underpinned our family life. We attended Mass every Sunday and were very interested in the personnel changes within the church structure as they would be pertinent to our family at least. As in any country town, there was a fair amount of talk about him and his ministry. Our family had a slight connection with him as his family had lived next door to my aunt and uncle in the 1940s and had shared a neighbourly friendship.

The priest's arrival at Christmas 1987 was welcome as the parish had been without a permanent priest for a while and the community, including the school, looked forward to a new order. His first Mass at Clarence Town was set down for Christmas Eve. It was raining and oversubscribed and we felt like sardines as we sat waiting for his debut appearance.

Minutes dragged by and then a good lady from the parish announced that Father had indeed arrived. We all smiled and forgot the discomfort as this was great news. It's not easy packing four boys aged eleven, ten, seven and three up and off to church on Christmas Eve. I'm sure they had other plans and hopes. Mothers and fathers also would have been considering the mountains of organising, cooking and assembling jobs parents do on this special night.

Another ten minutes went by and our good lady appeared again saying Father was indisposed and had suffered a gastric attack. I can tell you that at that moment, the number of people planning a Christmas communion plummeted. Good news soon after. Our friend reappeared and said Father was ready to begin and he had hurriedly commissioned the local school principal as a Minister of the Eucharist and she would be offering communion to the congregation. When Father took centre stage, so to speak, there was light clapping. He acknowledged this with a gracious nod. I'm not sure if he thought it was a welcome clap or realized that people were applauding his very wise decision to try and avoid contaminating his flock.

Father recovered from this inauspicious beginning and began to get to know his parish. Early on he announced from the pulpit that he liked cakes and sweets and was more than happy to accept them from good cooks. A bit of a strange message perhaps but for goodness sake he was the priest and if he liked cakes, then cakes he would have! He began to frequent the homes where he knew he would be made welcome and where there was a fair chance the food would be good. I remember teasing him about whether faith or food came first.

Father Fletcher's physical appearance reflected his love of cakes and sweets. He was overweight, had a very generous girth and an unhealthy pallor. He was forty-six years old, about five feet nine in height and had grey hair, which was sparse on top and brown eyes, watchful eyes. I didn't know that was a sinister thing until much later. I just thought he was always aware of the people in a room perhaps because he was slightly nervous when out of his comfort zone.

In hindsight, I know that he was calculating, judgemental and predatory. I wondered about the solitary tooth in his lower jaw but realised it was by choice, as he certainly could have enjoyed a subsidised visit to a dental prosthetic clinic. Remember, Catholic people looked after their priests. I wondered if he had rotted the other teeth with lollies or now I wonder, with the benefit of that same hindsight, whether there was something more disturbing about that single tooth. His jocular manner was selective and exaggerated when he chose and many people will remember that loud guffawing laugh. I remember that laugh one morning at our home when he laughed so hard at his own smutty interpretation of a comment that he nearly choked.

Daniel had suffered a really nasty bout of sore throat and swollen glands and a parishioner who had recently completed an alternative therapy medicine course, offered to come and 'balance' his bio rhythms. It sounds crazy now but it was an opportunity for her to practise her new skills. She said Daniel would get great benefit from the magic of her hands and besides, it was free. The priest had called in to see us and I chatted to him and hovered in and around Daniel's room as she worked on him. After a while she came out and solemnly declared "Well that went really well and I think all his organs should be up in the morning."

I thanked her and went to put the kettle on. I was stunned to hear the guffawing from the priest and eventually realised the cause of his smutty mirth as he reduced her innocent remarks to his own uncouth level. He spluttered and coughed and I am now sorry that I saved him with a drink of water. It actually was a poor choice of words on her part and the other boys may have smiled and winked at each other as young boys do, but it was entirely inappropriate for a priest to react like that.

A pattern of his social outings began to emerge. Families of boys welcomed him as he seemed to go out of his way to show interest in their lives. He was not a sportsman nor had ever been one but he knew what questions to ask the boys about the latest matches or cricket scores. To have a priest show a personal interest in you was pretty special in those days. As Daniel was achieving in so many areas, it was not surprising that he was singled out for this special interest. Many people complimented us on our boys and perhaps Daniel in particular, as he was the eldest and was the first to achieve many things.

Daniel was a very impressive young man and he was, as first born, our pride and joy. Comments from all manner of people who crossed his path about his sweet nature, his quiet conscientious dedication to family, schooling and sport were frequent. A sports writer described a particularly good cricket innings by Daniel, of 124 not out, as follows.

"He was impressive in everything he did. His footwork was impeccable and he hardly made a mistake all morning. But the thing that impressed me the most was the way he concentrated. He wasn't going to give his wicket away cheaply. He hit anything loose with the power of a player twice his size but when a ball was pitched in line with the stumps he met it with a defiant dead bat. The young fellow's name is Daniel Feenan and I'm sure you will hear more of him…"

School reports described him as "…a happy leader, a responsible role model and a caring and committed student who is a pleasure to teach…" The word, 'conscientious,' appeared on nearly every assessment. Such interest in our boy reinforced our delight in him and gave us the very reasonable expectation that he would continue on the successful pathway on which he had embarked.

He relished being given responsibility and so his generous disposition allowed him to be a wonderful brother and son. I remember him returning home from a shopping trip with his father and he had used all of his pocket money, which he had earned mowing our considerably large lawn, to buy me a rose in a cellophane cylinder. I still have the rose and he still has his generous nature. In hindsight, I can see that he was eager to please, but that shouldn't take on sinister perceptions as he was just a little boy, loving his family and being grateful for whatever privileges he was awarded as eldest son.

While remembering Daniel with warm pride, I cannot fail to mention his marvellous brothers. They were just as contented, loving and appreciative in so many individual and combined ways. The boys were very close, fiercely loyal to each other and were happiest when together. Whoever decided on a game to be played could rely on eager brothers to join in. They set about enjoying themselves with the minimum of fuss. Rules about what constituted a four or six in backyard cricket and what was the official try line in the footy games were quickly decided on. You see, living on a small farm, they did not have the luxury of being able to hop next door or across the road, if they didn't like the game being played at home. They quickly established the pattern for leisure time and played happily for hours. When friends arrived with their kids, the same games with the same conditions applied and the fun just happened. As adults now, they still laugh about sixes being hit into the goats' paddock or the swimming pool. No umpire needed there!

I remember when Father Fletcher asked us if Daniel could be an altar server, officially. He had served Mass on a few occasions before Father Fletcher arrived in the parish when the incumbent was unavailable. This duty had been performed by a couple of older men in the past, probably because there were no younger folk to take on the role. I expressed hesitation because I did not want to offend the men who were currently in the position. Father said that he would square it with them and that they were too old anyway.

He called in to say that Daniel had the guernsey and at that time, Luke showed interest and so he said they could both do it. He insisted that they were to wear soutanes (altar boy robes) and of course I sewed them with pride and diligence. Father had spoken and with my background of deference to a priest's wishes, I was only too happy to oblige. Moreover, I was very proud that he had singled them out for what was an important role in Church life.

When the boys said that Father had told them they didn't need to wear shirts under the robes, for coolness, I think I was appreciative that the priest was casual and understanding about the boys' dislike of formality. I now wonder if he was ogling both of them as they stripped their shirts off in the sacristy. This is a little room adjoining the altar in Catholic churches and it is where priests robe up for Mass and where the vases for the flowers and the brass cleaning gear is kept. I now know that the brass and silver weren't the only things tarnished in that little room.

It was about this time that Father asked me to be a Eucharistic Minister, a first for our parish. At that time, Dungog parish had two churches. One, St Mary's at Dungog, was the larger church and was located near the catholic primary school, convent and presbytery and the second one was St Patrick's at Clarence Town, a smaller church but closer to where we lived. I was humbled to be asked and protested that there were older and more fitting people who could carry out this special duty. I was shocked to hear him say that the local people were inbred and uneducated. I didn't agree and assured him that he probably had many well educated parishioners if he cared to get to know them.

His outlook and comment disturbed me. Nevertheless, I agreed to the suggestion that future faith development opportunities would flow from such a role and I accepted the position. I believe a male parishioner was inducted into the same role about this time but he was to be the Dungog Special Minister. We had a small ceremony at Mass soon after for it all to become official.

A sour note of the commissioning was the loud exit from the church of a female parishioner protesting my appointment. I only mention it to highlight the climate of resistance that existed, in that era, to change. My aged mother was there, very proud, and so was Father Fletcher's mother. A morning tea followed. This protesting lady was a neighbour of mine and Father promised to visit her and talk about her objections. He never did and this lady and her husband faded from the congregation.

A simple pastoral visit would have reassured them that the Church needed to involve lay people in the various ministries because of declining priest numbers. He wouldn't have got the cakes and he may have got some intelligent discussion but he chose to avoid the confrontation. They remained bitter but he still retained his idea that the priest's opinion would and should go unchallenged.

Power and self indulgence! There were other occasions where his power position might have been challenged and so we noticed how he managed situations. He avoided the places where he may have had to explain himself. The other families he befriended would know this. He praised us, pandered to our egos, sought advice that he didn't feel compelled to take and generally groomed the lot of us into thinking that we were special.

We formed an easy friendship with him and he seemed to get on well with the boys. We noticed that a lot of the families he became close to had sons. I saw nothing sinister in this and just came to a view that he related better to boys. He certainly took an interest in their lives. During the next two years, when Daniel and Luke had become official altar servers, I was asked to adopt various ministries within our church and as I seemed to have quite a few roles, I voiced my concerns to the priest about sharing the jobs among other parishioners. He flattered my ego with comments about me being the best person for the jobs and sometimes truthfully admitted that no-one else wanted them anyway. In keeping with my traditional catholic background, I continued to be very active in our church community. My most treasured ministry of all was taking communion to sick and elderly people. I felt humbled and honoured.

I remember taking communion, regularly, to an old couple who lived fairly close to the church. The dear old lady couldn't absorb the knowledge that I was Father's helper and used to say every Sunday,

"Well that's a pretty dress, Sister" as she had fixed in her head the opinion that I was a nun. She looked into my waiting family's car one day and commented on John and the boys. I explained they were my husband and four sons and she said she preferred the old days when nuns didn't marry. I tried with the explanation about Special Eucharistic Ministers helping the dwindling numbers of priests but it must not have been well understood as the very next week she said "Well that's a pretty blouse, Sister." Poor old souls probably went to God thinking that just too much had changed.

Visits to our home by the priest became commonplace because after all, there was much parish business and involvement to be discussed. He sometimes brought his mother with him and my own mother seemed to enjoy her company. The priest sought advice and opinion from John and me, puzzling us that he would do so. We asked ourselves on more than one occasion what he had done before coming to our parish and whether he had previous parishioners write his letters back to the diocesan office. I don't think either of us could have told him that we thought he was lazy. He was the priest. He had a pattern of visiting other families as well and probably flattered them into thinking that they were indispensable also.

I was raised in a traditional Catholic family and had enjoyed a Catholic education. Priests and nuns held exalted positions in our parishes and my family worked hard to see that "Father" had a decent presbytery to live in and "Sister" also need not be worried by financial hardship, manual labour or an inadequate classroom. Those were the years of fetes and parish balls to raise money to make these dutiful concessions to the religious a reality. Mum sewed aprons, struck plant cuttings in decorated pots and cooked hundreds of cakes and scones while Dad lost his voice year after year running the chocolate wheel as he cajoled the parishioners to buy a ticket.

I married a non-catholic man and, after twelve years of marriage, he made a commitment to the Church by becoming a Catholic. My two sisters, Christine and Moira, have similar stories with both their husbands converting to Catholicism after many years of marriage. I make this point only to highlight my opinion that the faith example shown by my sisters and myself encouraged the three men to want to experience the joy which we obviously gained from our faith.

Given my background, I can see that I was predisposed to supporting the priest and parish. I was a reader at Mass, church cleaner, member of and then chairperson of the parish council, convenor of Advent and Lenten groups and organiser of many meetings and assemblies in relation to the Renewal process in our diocese.

Strangely, after everything that has happened, I still miss the connection now and am lonely for the warmth of my faith.

4

The happy life continued and some of our visiting friends even contemplated emulating our particular recipe for rearing a happy family. Neighbouring properties were looked at and finances checked but no deals were done. By this time, our children were in upper primary school and secondary school was approaching. Issues of long bus travel and the idea of hours of homework became important. We too considered such issues but our love of our lifestyle and the boys' obvious happiness with their lives convinced us to stay.

Another consideration for us to continue living in the country was our involvement in our Catholic parish. By this time we had finally started to shake off the perception of us, by the local parishioners, as city dwellers and were now trusted with their friendships. It had been a slow apprenticeship with tentative greetings developing into enquiries about my new pregnancy and the birth and growth of the younger boys. I worked at the parish school at this time and that also helped with meeting people and bonding with families of similar persuasion. Weekly mass became a friendly affair with talk of the weather, cricket scores and vegetable gardens. Rainfall to our fellows meant a washout of their cricket while to our farming parishioners it was a godsend and there was much talk of inches fallen and the possibility of "follow up rain." I remember one of the boys asking what it was and why did everyone want it. It was a great lesson about 'the bigger picture'.

Father Fletcher was often at our place, eating dinner, having cups of tea and seeking opinions about how to manage some aspects of the parish. By this time, we had formed a parish council and I was a member and later became chair-person for about five years.

My husband had changed jobs and had been appointed to a newly created position of Financial Administrator of the Maitland Newcastle Diocese. A diocese is a geographical collection of parishes administered by a bishop. What kudos Fletcher sought from that appointment. He announced from the altar that he was very proud of John, it was going to be great to have a direct financial line to the bishop, and then he stuffed it up by saying that he himself was in no small way responsible for John getting the job because he "had made him what he is." It was said tongue in cheek but was insulting and demeaning and galling as we realised just how many letters we had written for him and how many balance sheets John had produced for him as a member of his Finance

Committee. A tally of hours given to meetings would be substantial. This was never a consideration until then because wasn't it a blessing to help out with whatever skills you had. Helping Father was akin to helping God.

As the years unfolded, some ominous clouds of uncertainty about our boys and Daniel in particular gusted across our particular sky. These caused us momentary unease but then were quickly dispersed because we believed that we, as a family, were strong and this strength was all we needed to manage life's traumas. Daniel's mood changes and occasional bursts of anger were surprising given his easy going nature, but not too worrying. Most of our friends had kids with mood issues and told us we were lucky to have had him with no temperament related incidents in his happy life until that stage.

Instead of the terrible two's he had a new little brother to play with and the naughty nines passed him by as he honed his cricket skills and ran free with three little brothers. In hindsight, this perception of ours that we were untouchable could be regarded as arrogant and in some aspects naive but we were trusting and trusted. Sure we had our disasters but didn't every family have those?

There was Dom's broken arm, nose, and the spill off the bike that Easter at the farm. There were no recriminations for a boy who had sped carelessly down the steep hill on the little bike because the sight of the doctor calmly scrubbing, with a toothbrush, the gravel from the huge tear on his knee sent sympathy shivers down everyone's spines. The laughing gas helped! I'm sure the doctor should have offered it to the mum and dad as well.

Accidents to visitors at our little farm were common-place as the kids ran wild over the paddocks, rode bikes at foolhardy speeds down the track with no helmets and often no shoes and then of course no skin on knees and elbows. When I bought food for the weekend guests, bandaids and antiseptic were also on the shopping list.

We had pneumonia on the ski fields. Try having warm air on a little boy in a caravan in minus three degrees. We had shingles on the eyelid at Movie World in Queensland. Try keeping sunglasses on a fourteen-year-old boy in Davey Jones' Locker which was a ride at the amusement park! The nebuliser worked well on the generated power on Fraser Island and I suppose the job of tester of all the amateur obstacle course equipment set up for a Help the Missions day at school showed school spirit at the outset and it was, after all, for charity. Being knocked unconscious was a minor inconvenience for one son and he did get a very special merit award from an embarrassed supervising teacher.

One of the more spectacular accidents was the crash through the roof of the little pool motor shed, by a boy doing acrobats on the pool fence. The flash of blue flame as a piece of the roof severed the power cable to the electric cell was scary and proved the absolute necessity for earth leakage protection as the amateur gymnast lay amongst the water and sheared off cable. I recall that we abandoned the planned tea and scones with a visiting nun and hooked straight into a stiff whisky. The sensational nature of that event always leads to a recall and reflection when the boys are reminiscing about their childhood. I am grateful that they have such incidents in their memories to laugh about. So much of their childhood has been tainted now.

5

Our boy was changing and we had no idea why.

When my father-in-law turned eighty, our family planned a birthday party for him at Adamstown, a suburb of Newcastle, where he lived. That was in December 1990. The evening went as planned until we realised that Daniel was missing. He had been playing cricket on the street with his brothers earlier and when they drifted into the backyard for the birthday cake he must not have come in with them. He wasn't missed for a while and when he was, we found it hard to comprehend and were alarmed. Some people at the party helped us search the neighbouring streets and John even popped his head into a few local pubs to see if he was there or anyone had seen a fourteen-year-old.

After about forty-five minutes, I rang the police and explained that this was a boy who was from the country and did not know his way around the suburbs of Newcastle.

The policeman said "Lady, every fourteen-year-old boy in Newcastle is missing at the moment because Jimmy Barnes is performing in the area and they are up trees and on fences trying to get a free look and listen!"

He also said if he didn't turn up in another hour to ring him back. We continued searching and calling and tried not to alarm the elderly relatives at the party. Not long after, Daniel came wandering up the street and we were very angry with him. Of course we asked him where he had been and he gave a weak excuse that he had gone into a neighbouring yard to retrieve a tennis ball and people came out on to the verandah and he was trapped. He said he didn't hear us calling and he must have dozed off.

We were never satisfied with this explanation but as he appeared very upset, we let it drop and packed up and went home with mixed thoughts. I believe his father and I thought that he might have given us a true statement away from the birthday crowd but that didn't happen. I remember he was very upset on the journey home and so were we as we had been very panicked by his absence.

The next morning at Mass, I told Father Fletcher about Daniel going missing and our concerns and worry and he said "Drop it Pat! Teenage boys, in my experience, often tried to show some independence and break out of the family activities." I could understand that there was some truth in this but then I knew Daniel would not want us to worry. We did not pursue the explanation but never forgot the uncharacteristic behaviour and indeed were able to recall the details of the night when asked by the police many years later. My own mother's diary entry and the Jimmy Barnes concert reference were very helpful in pinpointing the date of the party. Of course we knew the date of the old fellow's birthday, but not the exact date of the celebration.

School and sporting achievements continued for Daniel and his brothers. We spent many weekends watching cricket as the four of them played with local teams and then representative teams as well. A lot of washing and salad rolls and sun lotion and insect repellent are my memories of those busy times. It is just a fact that we were so busy but I would not change those happy family times for anything.

I love cricket. My grandfather was an excellent cricketer who took a hat trick "against the Poms," my husband enjoyed a long cricket career as a player and administrator and then we had those four sons who never tired of the game. On summer Sunday evenings, after a whole weekend on the cricket ovals, the boys could be found in the backyard batting and bowling as if they were playing for Australia.

Daniel's cricket talent scored him a place in a Hunter Valley team to tour New Zealand. We were so proud of him and thought that he would love the tour. We had discussed that he was often quiet and his old sunny nature was not as evident as it had been but put this down as a change towards his approaching manhood.

I remember two incidents about this time that were unusual and unexplained. One night, in the warmer months, my mother was minding the boys while John and I had an outing. I can't remember whether we slept away or returned home very late but the next morning she told us that Daniel had gone missing for a while the night before. Naturally we asked him where he had been. He said that he had taken the dog for a walk. We found this unusual, because we lived on a little farm and that meant the dog had plenty of exercise as she chased around after the boys. To my knowledge, none of the boys had ever taken her for a walk. He said that the dog ran off near a neighbour's party and it took him a while to retrieve her. It seemed reasonable but again a strange thing to do. We lived in the country and the neighbours were a fair hike away.

We were uneasy when the neighbour rang to say Daniel had been spotted near the party. The man was worried that one of the guests had frightened him in the very natural circumstances of quizzing him about his reasons for being there. There was some embarrassed smooth talking with the neighbours in question and mention of the inquisitive nature of fifteen-year-old boys was made. Apologies all round and we breathed a sigh of relief. Strange behaviour and again we would recall the incident in the future.

The other worrying thing at this time was the discovery that Daniel had lost a bag of his school clothes. We didn't miss them until the morning he was to leave on a tour of New Zealand. At that particular time, it was only the school shoes we missed as he needed to wear them as part of the tour uniform. We tore the house apart as we all searched and Daniel became sullen. The more we looked, the worse he got.

We left for the trip to the airport with mixed feelings. John was going as an accompanying adult and Luke was going as the chief supporter although he had hidden a set of cricket whites in the bottom of his suitcase just in case. Later in the tour, he did have a turn on a Kiwi wicket. Daniel was very upset on the way to Sydney and we couldn't understand his mood. The disappointment of the missing shoes shouldn't have caused such a reaction especially when he was able to wear an old pair.

As I thought about the missing shoes later that night when I returned from the airport, I realized that a whole bag of school uniform was missing. Daniel had a part time job at the local shop and he would change into work clothes after school at the shop when he got off the school bus. In the bag was a set of uniform, shorts, shirt, belt and shoes and of course we hadn't missed them as they must have gone missing in the last week of school before the Christmas break. Daniel hadn't needed any of them until the shoes were needed for New Zealand. I rang the bus company, the school when the holidays were over and we searched through the storeroom of the little shop. No clothes. I was very surprised when they turned up many weeks later at the school. Daniel seemed vague about the discovery but we were glad to get them back and accepted the story.

Another event we would recall in the future.

6

All the boys were growing and becoming individuals. They had their own friends, their own likes and dislikes and their own levels of motivation. These differences resulted in the need for them to be transported in many different directions, sometimes at the same time. We were very busy and these incidents, although unusual and worrying, did not really deter us from our mission of raising our sons in a respectful and loving environment. We laughed often and enjoyed one another.

The boys now say that they had a wonderful childhood surrounded by family and amazing friends. The ten cousins enjoy being together and are soon transported back to the days of cubby houses, treasure hunts, magic, river and creek adventures and all manner of exploits, some of which the mothers have never discovered. That's as it should be in normal families engaging in normal adventures whilst the mums, in this case, sisters, also delighted in each other. We happily prepared food for the multitudes and washed the results of the often muddy adventures. One niece said recently that the visits were fantastic and busy and the food just seemed to appear. She's a mother now and will no doubt discover the true story behind the appearance of afternoon tea. She'll learn how many sandwiches can be made from a loaf of bread and how far a tray of home baked biscuits will go.

We had a caravan through these years and enjoyed towing it around the eastern states in the school holidays and parking it near the beach every January. Those touring holidays are well remembered by my sons and the funny thing is that they often mention obscure parks in country towns where they bowled well or hit a six. Spilling out of the car when we had a lunch break, they would play cricket until a meal was ready, and then they'd pile back into their seats and sleep until the next stop. I am much happier knowing they remember the games and fun rather than the Big Banana or the Dog on the Tuckerbox.

Daniel was a very hard worker at school and seemed to look forward to these breaks. In term time he often suffered from headaches and moodiness and we thought this was due to the high standards he had set for himself in all areas of his life. He spent more time in his room away from the family. When he would join in with his brothers, he was often over-exuberant but the boys would be delighted to get the old Daniel back.

They will no doubt remember him running around the house with an onion bag on his head saying, "Buy a wok for your mother!" a spoof of an ad on television at that time. Looking back now with the benefit of hindsight, I can see the depression and confusion lifting for short bursts when he would become carefree again, especially when we were on holidays away from home.

Through all these times, our priest commented that the mood changes were part of growing up. We were uneasy because the other boys were growing up too and did not suffer from the same anxieties and mood swings. They were just normal and on one hand, the detentions and unsatisfactory exam results were nothing out of the ordinary although irritating. On the other hand, Daniel did not like to fail anything, set himself lofty standards and never really gave us a reason to discipline him. That made it harder to negotiate responsibility and consequences with him when he began socialising in sometimes inappropriate ways.

School was eventually over for Daniel and he seemed to enjoy that first summer of freedom. He looked forward to commencing university the following year and I recall that we hoped he would settle down to the new regime of study with the opportunity of self-regulation that didn't really exist for him at school. We were concerned at the way Daniel was proceeding to experience his away-from-school freedom and spoke to him about moderation in drinking among other things. His mates seemed to be doing similar things so we tried not to worry too much, but we were very uneasy.

In February 1995, just two days before Daniel was to start university, he had a fall while out drinking with some mates and finished up in hospital with a fractured skull. He underwent surgery for an extradural haematoma and was in a serious condition for a few days before he made a good recovery, from a medical point of view. Years later, Father James Fletcher could not recall going to the hospital's intensive care ward and anointing Daniel while giving him the Blessing of the Sick. We remembered his visit and it was recorded in the medical notes.

However, the disappointment of a late start at uni, the premature end to that season's cricket for Daniel and the debilitating loss of fitness caused him to be severely depressed. As my boy started to struggle with his life for the next twelve months, we were inclined to blame the head injury but it became evident that there were other causes of his mood swings, poor concentration and general unhappiness.

As an aside, Dominic told me recently that he had suffered from a broken finger at the time of Daniel's accident and we were too upset to notice. Sorry Dom.

7

The next months were a mixture of good times and bad but we were becoming very anxious about Daniel's inability to slow down and make good decisions about driving, drinking and general commitment to improving his lifestyle. He had a couple of worrying car accidents when he drove late at night after working long hours. The friction at home was mounting as he lived life close to the edge. As he continued to take risks, we couldn't understand why he didn't seem to value his life. This was not the son I had known and I found it very hard to watch as he started to go off the rails. In September 1995, he came home from work and he had been drinking. At that time he was working for a neighbour who was a concreter and he seemed to enjoy the outdoor life. There were early starts, hard work and often early-afternoon finishes. I'm sure Daniel appreciated the easygoing mateship of his boss and the uncomplicated days and he certainly learned much about the trade.

However, hard work like that is often accompanied by hard drinking and Daniel embraced that side of it as well. On that day in September when he arrived home, I was sick with pneumonia and sick of seeing him wobble up the paddock so I let him know of my displeasure. We had a short heated exchange and I went back to bed. I heard the back door slam and lay for a few minutes wondering where he was going.

The anxious feeling that was becoming more prevalent returned and after a moment I decided to check on what he was doing. I walked up to our farm shed and saw Daniel standing on a trailer beside the tractor. He had strung up a noose and I screamed. He jumped.

I grabbed his legs and wouldn't let go as I supported his weight. I don't know how long I stood there screaming but after a while he stopped kicking at me and started to cry. I heard the school bus pull up at our front gate and yelled for Bernard, eleven-year-old Bernard, to help. Bernard heard me screaming and rushed to the shed.

He climbed up while I continued to support Daniel's weight. He undid the rope from around his brother's neck allowing Daniel to lower himself to the ground. He told me he was sorry and went down to the house with his little brother. I collapsed against the tractor wheel and sobbed hysterically.

We gathered at the house and I rang John and he drove straight home rather than going to the meeting he had planned to attend. We realised that Daniel needed help and talked to him about seeking someone to talk to. We were at our wits' end to know what to do – so guess who we rang!

Father James Patrick Fletcher.

The priest had been moved to a new parish at Branxton. I talked to him and told him what had happened and he asked if we would bring Daniel up to his presbytery at Branxton and he would talk to him. He explained that he couldn't come to us as he had visitors but said that he would get rid of them. Although Daniel was still intoxicated, he said he would keep him all night so he could have a long talk to him and I asked Daniel if he would go. He agreed and so John drove him up. I rang our family doctor who expressed concern about the whole situation and he said he would come up and see us as soon as John arrived home from Branxton. This kind man talked to us for hours and said he would see Daniel on the Monday to try and work out what was going on with him.

Daniel rang John the following morning and asked to be picked up. He was very upset and of course we put it down to his suicide attempt. He had an ugly bruise and welt encircling his neck and they were visible for quite a few weeks. The sinister cause of his obvious grief emerged years later.

Daniel did see our doctor who referred him to a psychiatrist, as he believed he was suffering from depression. He was advised to reduce his alcohol intake and we hoped that he might heed the advice of a non-family member.

He continued to work for a concretor, did bar work at night and had a girlfriend. All normal enough activities for a young fellow but his heavy drinking was starting to affect him in the usual ways. He hated us to talk to him about it and there were many rows. We couldn't understand why he was so angry and still wondered if there were residual issues from his head injury. I remember one night before Luke's school formal when Daniel lashed out at us in anger and we went to the dinner, sad, frustrated and disappointed for Luke as it was supposed to be his big night.

The New Year, 1996, had us hoping for peace and no more worry. We could clearly see the disparity between our two elder boys' behaviour and we couldn't explain it at all. Luke socialised with his friends often but there were no incidents and accidents and most of all no bad, angry behaviour.

University started and Daniel began a new course. He kept trying, I believe, but it was obvious that something was wrong. He passed his subjects but decided to defer the second semester. He and his girlfriend split up and he increased his bar work and other part-time employment. He seemed to listen when we tried to talk to him but was reluctant to change his lifestyle.

We begged him to consider his future and cease the binge drinking that so often caused his bad behaviour. But he didn't moderate his drinking and decided to move out from home in the next few months. We helped him move, hoping that a new and independent lifestyle might encourage responsibility, but he was only gone a week or two when he had a drink driving charge. He lost his licence and we embarked on a 'drive him to work' regime. We thought with all his traumas, it was important to support him in holding down a job.

By this time he was working for a landscaper and we thought the open air and hard work were ingredients for success. In hindsight, it wasn't our responsibility to get him to work and it might have encouraged him to escape the consequences of his bad behaviour further, but we were burdened by the memory of the suicide attempt and felt we had no choice. So drive we did. It was about an hour and a quarter round trip, if we didn't strike heavy traffic.

He came home for Christmas and never went back to the flat to live. In January, he packed up quickly, dumped everything on the bedroom floor and went off on a cricket tour with his father. Naive little mother that I was, I hummed happily as I washed and lovingly folded his clothes back into the cupboard of his childhood.

Mother bear was happy!

8

Daniel had played well on the cricket tour and returned looking well and settled. However, there were further problems with his drinking and we worried about him quite a bit. It was a different sort of worry when he announced that he had met a lady who was very nice, but seven years older than him and who had two children. Daniel was twenty at the time and his problems were still evident.

Initially we were horrified that he was taking on so much responsibility so young, but he seemed to be happy and settled into the domestic scene quickly. He continued to work and we gradually became used to the new little family. We helped them move to a different home and I tried not to be judgmental, as John and I laboured with boxes of toys and crockery while she strutted through the mess dressed in a short white dress and very high black sandals. I remember saying waspishly to John, "What's the matter with shorts and joggers like us?"

During the time Daniel was living with Belinda, they decided to move to Nelson Bay, a lovely coastal area. Her mother lived there and could help with babysitting if she could get a job. The little girls were about five and seven. The couple struggled with their finances and employment for her was vital if they were going to move ahead at all. It was a bit of a hopeless situation really and I had quite a few phone calls from her as she objected to Daniel's drinking patterns.

His twenty-first birthday was a small family celebration with a couple of close friends. We have a photo of him cutting his cake with the two little girls, one on each knee. It wasn't quite the celebration we had in mind for our eldest son. He was only fourteen years older than the eldest little girl.

On one memorable evening, I was at a parish council meeting and received a call from John to say that Daniel had turned up at the Nelson Bay presbytery and was drunk and abusive. The parish priest was worried and didn't know what to do. I was half an hour away in the opposite direction so John rang a friend to drive him over – he himself had had a few drinks and couldn't drive. Meanwhile, I rang the priest, not Father Fletcher but the one complaining about Daniel, and asked him to ring the police. He told me that Daniel was shouting out some weird things about priests and sex.

Interestingly, I remember when I mentioned to the priest at the meeting I was attending that night that I was upset and told him about the latest incident with Daniel, he said he couldn't help me as he was "off duty" at 9.30. It was then 9.45 pm. It didn't seem to occur to him that I had just driven thirty minutes to run his parish council meeting on a week night and that I had worked all day.

Years later, when the abuse allegations came out, Daniel explained what had set him off that night. That day, Daniel was at the local RSL club at lunchtime with Belinda and was noticed by the parish priest of Nelson Bay and a fellow priest who were having lunch together. The second priest knew Daniel quite well; he had often been around when we socialised with one particular family who were close friends of the priest. Later when Belinda left, the two priests spoke to Daniel and asked him what he was doing with his life. One of them made the smart comment that the trouble with Daniel was that he was not thinking with his head but rather "with his dick." Although such a comment from a man might not normally be particularly offensive, coming from a man of the cloth it was unusual to say the least. I guess that Daniel drank on with the comment festering away and finally found himself at the fellow's presbytery angry, indignant and upset. Years later, when that particular priest was asked to provide a statement to police describing that very telling incident, he baulked. On the Friday, he was willing to go and give a statement but on the Monday, he did not turn up at the police station. When asked to explain, he said that really, Daniel was only saying that his parents didn't understand him. Poor memory, or influenced in some way or just plain gutless?

Both Belinda and Daniel decided to seek work in Sydney and in fact, Daniel landed a good job with Westpac. They moved and it wasn't very long before the relationship ended.

Perhaps Daniel looked around to see what other twenty-two-year-olds were doing with their lives. Certainly not enduring a long train trip home to the western suburbs and then sitting up with home readers and homework activities with their partner's children.

I remember the day that my youngest son and I drove, full of hope, to Sydney to help Daniel move to another home. It was a day of uninterrupted torrential rain and not much daylight. I collected him from a mate's place in the inner city at Alexandria and then we drove to Blacktown to collect the rest of his possessions. He had moved out about a fortnight before and had found a great place to rent over in Manly. So, still smiling but getting a little grimfaced by then, because I was driving in such terrible conditions, we set out for the new abode, loaded to the gunnels with his gear. After a few hours, we left him waving us goodbye from the footpath after settling him in and having a very late lunch at a lovely pub in Manly.

It was a long trip home but happy enough as I mused optimistically about his new direction and that he had distanced himself from the wholly mad notion that he could be the head of a family of four at the age of twenty two years.

9

It wasn't long before Daniel was telling us about employment opportunities in Tasmania. The bank was setting up a new call centre in Launceston and Daniel was keen to go there. We were pleased about the career advancement and supported his new venture. We were certain he had the potential and personality for a great career in dealing with the public and hoped that the new position was the beginning. Gradually we began to hear of a girl who was also going to the Apple Isle and we correctly guessed that she was influential in Daniel's decision to go. More carting of stuff down to him was carried out in preparation for his departure. I remember taking his golf clubs and a BIG cricket bag in the luggage compartment of the bus I was travelling on with forty other women for a shopping weekend. Daniel collected his gear from our hotel in the next few days.

Our whole family had a beautiful last day with him in Sydney. We travelled on the ferry over to Manly and had a great meal together and then we journeyed to the airport to say farewell. It was a lovely day and we were all so happy for Daniel and had such positive hopes that he would move forward.

The last few months of 1998 passed quickly and without any worries about our eldest son. The news from Tasmania was always positive and we gradually relaxed and thought the worst was over. We had learned that his new partner was eight years older than he was and knew that she would probably be ready to settle down sooner than he would be, but that wasn't really a worry at all.

We had sold our home in November and were busy packing and planning our new home, which was to be built in the area but on a smaller block of land. Our other sons were progressing with career, university and school and we were happy. Our second son celebrated his twenty-first birthday with a great party and we were very proud of his achievements and told him so in our speeches. Daniel's lifestyle had affected all the boys and we were mindful that they all be given the chance to shine. Dominic had just completed his HSC and was hoping to study in Canberra. We were sad he might be leaving us but delighted that he had a good idea of the direction he wanted his life to take. Presents arrived from Tassie for the twenty-first and for Christmas. I realised that Daniel was also forward planning and that was cheering in itself.

Daniel started playing cricket in Launceston and had lots of funny cricket stories to tell us. John, Bernard and I had a holiday in Tasmania where we met Kim, the girlfriend, and we took a little tour around the countryside. We were thrilled to see Daniel looking well but a little anxious that he seemed to be drinking heavily at times. Kim complained about him a fair bit and said that she loathed cricket so I wondered about their future. They became engaged a few months later and I concluded that together, they had worked out their issues. They began to plan their wedding and Daniel asked Father Fletcher if he would come to Tasmania to marry him. I've naturally wondered about that since. When I asked Daniel, "What was your idea in wanting that man to perform the ceremony?" he said that he wanted Fletcher to look at him and know that he, Fletcher, had lost him forever to Kim.

Fletcher refused to travel to Tasmania saying that he was frightened to fly over water. I remember offering to drive him down and he said there would be a lot of paperwork to complete as the wedding was in a different state and he would need to get permission from the cardinal. I doubt the truth of this because I was told later that he was happy to travel to Western Australia to visit his sister and carry out priestly duties there. I thought it was a pathetic excuse and told him so but I didn't push the paperwork angle as I decided that if it was too much trouble for an old friend, then we didn't want him there anyway. We still didn't know what had occurred between him and Daniel, so his refusal of such an important role left us feeling very disappointed.

He rang one day and asked if I could call up to Branxton so that he could give me a sample of some pew decorations for Daniel's and Kim's wedding. Then he'd be there in spirit, he said. I did go up and he produced an arrangement of tulle and ribbon, in black, for me to take down to Daniel on my next visit. I remember saying it was a wedding not a funeral and he said he didn't think Daniel would worry about the colour. Hindsight is great, but was he sending Daniel a not-so-subtle message?

The pew decorations were not needed however as the engagement was called off. Daniel was very upset but Kim said she couldn't marry him as he was difficult when he drank. There had been a few episodes when he showed his underlying anger and distress and we came to realise that Daniel had trouble maintaining relationships because of this. Over the next few months, we all travelled separately to see him as we were using up the air tickets we had purchased for the wedding.

He flew home for a family wedding near Moree in the March and it was a magic time. The ten cousins rejoiced in being together and we all enjoyed a fantastic country wedding. There was some solid drinking over that Easter and I can honestly say that Daniel, for a change, wasn't the worst offender. When we gather now, the stories flow and we laugh again about the really funny incidents that probably happen at all home weddings. It was a happy family occasion and timely and I thought Daniel would reconnect with all the people who were special to him. He did and I was truly happy for him.

But I was also sad that a definite rift was beginning to widen between his father and myself. This story is not about my other pain; however, my husband's hectic work schedule, self-medication with alcohol for his pain and our emotional exhaustion from worrying about Daniel definitely contributed to the marriage breakdown. We separated in November 2000. Since the family wedding in March, we had worried about Daniel as his life spiralled out of control again. Quite a few of his friends in Launceston rang us and expressed concern about his lifestyle. A new relationship had also ended.

After all our hopes, it appeared that Daniel's life was again spiralling out of control.

10

On the 4th of December 2000, Daniel rang from Tasmania to say that he had been off work and was very stressed. When I asked him why, he said it was because of our marriage break-up and other things. He said he had seen a doctor and had been referred to a psychiatrist. I told him I thought that it was a good move as it was obvious he had been having problems for years, had unexplained anger and whatever the matter was, it needed fixing. Daniel agreed and then there was silence.

I cannot explain why – call it what you will – but I had a moment of mother's intuition and said "Daniel, I want to ask you something and I want you to give me an honest answer. Have you ever been sexually abused?" I had fretted and searched for an explanation of his behaviour for some time and perhaps that was the one question that I had not asked before. After a short silence he whispered "Yes." I was stunned and asked him "Can you tell me about it?" Through tears he said "I have trouble getting over it and I will go along for a while and then it will come back to haunt me." "Of course it will!" I declared indignantly," Who hurt you?" He said "I don't want to tell you over the phone but when I come home this Friday, I will talk about it then." I told him I loved him and he said that he loved me too and then we ended our conversation.

I sat on my bed trying to work out why I had asked that particular question. I wondered who, where and how and also about the degree of seriousness. The boys had often accused me of being over-protective and so I was particularly puzzled at the 'how.' From what I knew of sexual abuse victims, I realized that Daniel fitted the profile with his anger and excesses, his mood swings, lack of confidence and lack of abiding self-respect. I cried for Daniel. Luke was home that night and after a while, I went and told him what Daniel had just said. He stared at me for about thirty seconds and then started to cry, saying that he believed that was exactly what was the matter with his brother and why on earth hadn't we thought of it before. Brotherly vibes perhaps added to his professional health background.

When Luke went home, I rang both my sisters and told them what Daniel had said. Through all their nephew's traumas, they had been loving and unstinting in their support of me and they had both tried to talk to Daniel many times. One lived near Moree and one in Sydney and they both suggested that the abuser would be Father Jim. I was astounded.

Separately, they both said that they thought the intensity of Fletcher's interest in their nephew had been unusual. I thought of other possible people who had been in Daniel's life but acknowledged that the priest had always been very interested in him. The next morning I rang his father, he came to the house and we had a coffee and talked about the latest news. We were in no doubt that something had caused our son to struggle with his life. I had never been able to understand or source his anger and I couldn't reconcile myself to the knowledge that he just didn't seem to care about himself when, to our knowledge, he had every reason to be very proud of his achievements. I started to think about Father Fletcher.

Sexual abuse could explain his pain. John and I had been apart for a month and most of our conversations still figured Daniel. It was overwhelming because we knew something was wrong with him but up until then, we had no idea of the cause and so there had been no chance of a cure. At least we now knew the reason and we were very anxious to learn who the abuser was.

When Daniel came home the following Friday he said the abuse had happened and he agreed he needed professional help. He said he wasn't prepared to give details and that was frustrating but we had to respect his wishes. He had a night out with Luke and Dominic and they all came home in a taxi about 2am. I know the boys were hoping he might tell them something of the abuse.

They were all so emotional that they began to argue and then Daniel broke down and cried that he had been raped when he was younger. The boys and I were upset and tried to calm him down but he was much more upset than we were and threatened violence, an immediate return to Launceston and suicide.

Dom rang the police after Daniel became more violent to say we needed help. However, Luke was able to sit out on the front verandah near Daniel and use his health related expertise to talk Daniel down out of the rage. Dom and I decided that it would be best if the police didn't come so poor Dominic hurried up to the corner to flag them down and tell them that we didn't need them after all. I succeeded in talking to the police myself by phone and said Luke had mental health experience and was making a good job of calming his brother. They agreed to abort the callout but gave me a direct number to ring if things didn't improve.

Daniel eventually agreed to go to bed, thanks to Luke's wisdom and skill, and then I walked up to the corner and told Dominic the crisis was over. He was cold, upset and by then, completely sober. It was about 4 am. The boys told me they were going to Branxton the next morning with two bricks to deal with the person who had assaulted their brother although they had promised Daniel not to tell me.

I was anxious that they might take it into their heads to drive if they woke in the night, so I gathered all the car keys and hid them. I spent the rest of the night sitting bolt upright in bed, listening for any sound that might indicate that the boys were awake and that the fuss would start again. The next morning the boys told me that Daniel had confirmed our suspicions: Father Fletcher was the one who had assaulted him. He also informed them that it had taken place on the night of his suicide attempt when he had been taken up to Branxton Presbytery. I was appalled. Daniel confirmed the story to me when he woke and he said he didn't want to talk about it at that stage.

John, Luke, Dominic and I took him to the airport when he went back to Tasmania and urged him to seek professional help. We also stressed that we loved him and that we would support him in whatever way he wanted. Disclosing the abuse to us had been a monumental leap for Daniel and we understood that he didn't want the police involved at that stage.

He had a few very rocky months after that and we learned he was sinking into debt as he drank and gambled. There was no steadying influence in his life down there. He decided to transfer to Brisbane, packed up what few possessions he still owned and drove home. He called in and had one night with me on his way up the coast. I did try to talk to him about the abuse but he was reluctant and I let the matter drop. We completed a sorting out of his clothes and I found myself back in the laundry, washing and folding but not humming at all. I will forever hate those red and blue striped plastic bags which were always used by Daniel in his 'running away' years. I have gathered them from many abodes and on many occasions a knock on the door preceded Daniel and his bags as he moved home yet again. Sometimes the bags just arrived but without Daniel for a day or so.

I had been given three little saplings and hadn't planted them. We shared a good half an hour together while he planted them with me.

As they have grown, I have watched them and in some way, they have been a connection to my pained son. I watered them regularly so they would survive and they are tall and strong.

He left the next morning and I hoped that a change might be good. Of course, I lent him the money for the accommodation bond on a new flat.

On Friday the 13th April 2001, at about 2.00am, I had another upsetting phone call from Daniel. He said he had hurt himself by throwing himself under a small truck and was at a hospital north of Brisbane. He was very distressed, drunk and in shock and said he couldn't keep going. He had tried unsuccessfully to reach his father. He asked me to try and then his phone went dead. I did reach his father and discovered that he had a girlfriend and was sleeping over at her place. Pain. Double pain.

It was Good Friday and I spent a miserable day although the friends I reached out to were wonderfully supportive. A niece and her husband arrived from Sydney as planned for Easter and she capably assumed the role of hostess, poor kid. I cried all day; it was certainly a low point in my life. Apparently, I said more than once that it was a very Black Friday and that became a source of black humour to at least one of my sons. It has paled into insignificance for me as the terrible truth about the abuse has unfolded.

Daniel eventually rang in the afternoon and said he was bruised and cut but okay. I asked him to come home and sort his problems out and he said he would get help.

School holidays were on and so on the following Friday I fled to my sister's farm at Warialda, which is in the north west of New South Wales, with my youngest son. We were all upset. John rang on the Sunday to tell me that Daniel now had a DUI (driving under the influence) charge and had spent the night in the lock-up in Brisbane. When released, he drove home to find the police waiting at his flat and they arrested him again. When the police let him go, he found a doctor who directed him to the Royal Brisbane Hospital's psychiatric ward. Daniel had walked for an hour to get there and admitted himself. He was in a poor state, mentally and emotionally.

My sister and I drove to Brisbane the next day. It was a really long drive through south-western Queensland and we had plenty of time to talk. John had flown up but he left before we arrived on the Monday evening. Daniel was pleased to see us but he was very upset. He told us he was seeing a psychiatrist, and he was very upset that he couldn't manage his life. No great revelation there. He told me he had mentioned the abuse to the doctors and he felt a load had been lifted off his shoulders.

My sister Christine and I stayed with a cousin of John's and the family was welcoming, loving and very supportive. We visited Daniel each day, I bought him some new clothes and then when he seemed relatively settled, we decided to leave to drive back to the farm. I felt I was deserting him but his doctor said he would be there for a while and I knew he was safe enough. He was having alcohol and drug counselling and some help to look into his unmanageable life.

When Daniel was released from hospital, he only lasted one night and then rang me and asked if he could come home and live with me. I suggested he wait until his court appearance for the drink driving charge and he said he couldn't. John flew up and drove him and his little ute home and they arrived the day before Mothers' Day, 2001. When he went to bed that night, he called me into his room, thanked me and said that he felt safe at last. Ever the optimist, I believed that things would work out for him and he would settle and manage his life better.

Daniel and I flew to Queensland at the end of May, courtesy of John's frequent flyer points. He was very anxious about his court appearance and when he was fined and his licence was revoked, he believed it was fair treatment. He thanked me for not turning my back on him and said he would talk about the abuse when he was ready. He also said we wouldn't understand and so I asked him to trust us and that we would never desert him. He said he did trust us but thought he had dealt with the abuse himself. I knew he was still struggling but could only let him know that I loved him and would be there when he needed me.

Daniel slept all the way home in the plane and I watched him for most of that time. Not for the first time I wondered where our strong and confident young man had gone and how was I ever to help this frightened and insecure Daniel who needed so much support.

Where was the Year 10 school captain, All Round Academic Achiever, elite cricketer, 'chick magnet' (according to his brothers), and generally happy and strong son?

11

Daniel found work and settled down reasonably well. He started a new relationship and seemed happy enough but it wasn't long before the old demons started to torment him again. The old patterns resurfaced and there was another broken relationship and poor self-esteem issues underneath his reasonably confident outward appearance.

Late in 2001, he applied for a good job in Newcastle and succeeded in getting it. He still talked in general terms about the abuse and said that no one should have to have put up with what he had and of course we agreed notwithstanding the fact that we really didn't know any details. More drinking but good progress at work followed and we all started to hope that he was on the improve. A new relationship with a lovely lady named Donna with two small children began and he settled down really well. Fingers crossed. When I first met Donna, she asked me if I minded Daniel being with someone who already had two children. I remember saying to her that if she was the person who could make Daniel happy and settle down, then I would be very grateful and the children were a bonus. She looked me straight in the eye and said, "You're looking at her!"

She was a sweet and bubbly person who obviously wanted the best life possible for her children and I was impressed with her determination to make that happen. She told me that Daniel had told her of his problems and she believed that together they could overcome them. I breathed a sigh of relief, yet again, and tried to relax. Of course not any of us, including Donna, had any notion of the stress that was waiting to engulf us and test us to the very limits of our endurance and resilience. An unexpected pregnancy developed and Daniel was over the moon with happiness.

I was visiting a sick aunt with my mother when Daniel rang. He told me his new partner's mother was in the same hospital and so I decided to seek her out and meet her as were going to be the grandmothers of the coming baby. I met Donna's parents and they told me what a fine fellow Daniel was but they did think he drank a bit much at times. Donna had apparently been going to ring Bernard, who was eighteen, to get Daniel one night in recent times. My feelings were of disappointment and anger and they began to accelerate.

In the evening after meeting Donna's parents, I had been invited to the home of friends for dinner. I remember being distracted through the evening, so much so that my friend said she thought I was ill. I was thinking of Daniel all through that night and remembering how many times we had picked him up and guided him forward.

Later at home, I tossed and turned as I realised that the new relationship, although seemingly happy, was suffering the same problems as earlier ones. I was so disappointed that the drinking was still an issue. However, I had been around alcohol-related problems for a long time and understood very well that drinking was so often a way of coping with deep-seated distresses in a person's life.

I eventually fell asleep and when I woke on the Sunday morning, I had a new resolve. Daniel would have to stand alone with his alcohol-related behaviour and Bernard would not be rescuing him and bringing him home to sober up. I phoned Donna's home and asked if I could go and talk to them both. When I arrived and stated my mission very clearly to Daniel, he was very defensive. We talked about the new baby coming, Daniel's own child, and the importance of stability for Donna's two children.

Daniel became upset. He told me that he would be going along all right with his new resolve and then memories and anger would derail him and he would find himself back on the merry-go-round of destructive behaviours that were impeding his life. I remember grabbing hold of him and physically shaking him, saying it just had to be over as we were all sick to death of the long miserable journey of watching our beloved son self destruct.

I asked Daniel what it would take to wipe the slate clean and he said he had thought he might talk to the police. An overwhelming feeling of relief swept over me, as I knew I had exhausted every available option and I hoped there would be a great weight lifted from our shoulders if someone else could help our son. He said he was ready to talk. I phoned John, his father, and asked if he would come up to where we were as Daniel was thinking of going to the police about the abuse. He came immediately. Daniel explained to him that he thought the abuse was having a bad effect on his life and of course we were all in agreement with that.

So there we were, sitting around a table, having a coffee and thinking of the past and that one incident at Branxton Presbytery about seven years before. We believed Dan when he had previously disclosed the abuse but we were puzzled about the motivation of the priest. There was so much that we still didn't know.

Soon after the original disclosure about that night, in 2000, John had asked Bishop Michael Malone whether there had been any "previous form" with Fletcher, meaning of course if there had been any suggestion of inappropriateness with young males. He looked up his file and told John there was nothing in it that would indicate any such thing. He was the bishop so of course John believed him. Years later, we discovered that the bishop had had a meeting in February 1997 with a school principal about possible issues with Fletcher and young boys. As time went by, we learned that this sort of cover-up wasn't unusual.

We were all a bit emotional as we talked and John said to Daniel that he supported and loved him but he couldn't understand why the priest would abuse him suddenly when he was nineteen years old. My beloved son looked at me, tears welling in his eyes and said that it was because it had started when he was twelve years old.

Silence, at first. Then noise, the deafening noise in my head. I was screaming in silence as I recognised the truth, the horrible, unpalatable truth. Images of Daniel and his brothers laughing with the priest, John and I talking with the priest and then memories of Daniel's distress flashed and collided with one another in my head. I wept. We all wept.

Daniel's father and I both spoke at the same moment with the same thought. When? We knew that, to our knowledge, the priest had had no opportunity to seek Daniel's company without our being aware of it. I had no understanding of a paedophile's scheming or execution of his craft. I now know that as a paedophile, this man was the 'complete unit' – the technical name for a 'full-blown' paedophile.

He groomed his victims, manoeuvred, offended and covered his tracks with precision and arrogance. He of course created opportunities away from us in Maitland where Daniel attended secondary school. And there were those chances when he drove Daniel between our parish churches as an extra altar server. For Christ sake, he was in between celebrating Masses! I had a horrible premonition that some of those earlier puzzling instances involving Daniel would now be explained. I had no idea what pain we were all about to go through as Daniel revealed his journey of abuse and survival. Daniel's pain would be ongoing and there would be a new journey that he and his family would now be making together.

I rang a very old and trusted friend in the legal profession whom I knew would help Daniel start the journey. He was very kind and concerned and told Dan that he would set up a meeting with a policeman whom he respected and who would treat Daniel with respect as well. He told Daniel he would ring him the next day with a time and place. I have no idea what the others did, but I spent the afternoon looking at old photos, crying and asking, 'Why?'

That night, I happened to be watching television and there was an interview between Richard Carlton and Cardinal George Pell on Sixty Minutes about clergy sexual abuse in the Catholic Church and the way in which the victims were treated. There were parents being interviewed and they talked about the way the abuse affected their children. I had a hope that Daniel wouldn't be watching as he had been very upset earlier in the day. No. He was watching and for the first time he saw himself as a victim because he could identify with the sort of behaviour and life difficulties that other victims had experienced.

He told me some time after, that up until that point, he just felt he kept stuffing up because of bad decisions. He couldn't understand that his mates drank and socialised and lived rather normal lives but when he did that, there were often very serious consequences. He hadn't factored in post-traumatic stress, anger and confusion. That night he recognised a pattern of behaviour that he was very familiar with. The paedophile priest, Father Fletcher, had done a comprehensive job in warping Daniel's mind into believing that the relationship he had had with him was somehow Dan's fault. The load of guilt that my boy had carried was heavy and unfounded.

It was all too much and Daniel exploded by telephoning Father Fletcher. Father Fletcher, the parish priest, the family friend, the paedophile. On hearing Fletcher's voice, Daniel let loose and held nothing back in telling this man, this pitiful excuse for a priest, what he thought of him. It probably wasn't the thing to do on the eve of going to the police. The outburst left Daniel upset and angry, but he said that it had made him feel better and for the very first time in his long association with the priest, the power was about to turn. Interestingly, Fletcher didn't realise it was Daniel on the phone so one might wonder who else he thought it might be.

Strangely, he didn't ring the police after such an abusive phone call but called up one of his fellow priests to go and stay with him.

12

On 3rd June 2002, Daniel and Donna had their first meeting with Detective Sergeant Peter Fox who became our trusted friend and rock over the ensuing few years.

I remember praying, still did it, for Daniel that this meeting with the police would help him start on a path to recovery. We were very careful not to badger him with questions although there were a million we longed to ask. The main one of course was why he hadn't told us, followed closely by when and where it had happened. The whole upset was exacerbated by the fact that John and I had separated and perhaps one of the underlying causes was because we had run out of emotional fortitude as we had watched our eldest son living a self-destructive lifestyle. Here we were again, having long conversations about him but this time with a clear insight as to what the problem was.

My circle of trusted people, who had known about Daniel's original allegation of abuse suffered at Branxton

Presbytery, were stunned at the latest allegations but completely convinced of the truth of Daniel's story as they reflected on his past traumas and difficulties with life. I had cried on shoulders many times in the past and they had not forgotten.

My two sisters and their families are very special women who have shouldered our burden and walked the journey with us, sometimes carrying me when the load became too heavy and never refusing a conversation or plea for help to make sense of the latest evil. All this support was given unconditionally through times in their busy lives as they worked full time and managed their own family commitments. My other relatives and friends know exactly who they are and I hope they are aware of the wonderful support and contribution they have given to me. My respect for their privacy is the reason they won't be named in this story but I can assure each one that they will be in my grateful heart forever as I reflect on the company, meals and encouragement they have all shared with me. In my many lonely times, they were only a phone call away and time with them, while not minimising the terrible situation I had found myself in, helped considerably in reminding me that there was a normal, beautiful world embracing me.

After Daniel's first visit to the police, we held our breath. We had no idea what was ahead nor of the time it would take to walk that particular path. I remember his first visit was on a Monday, and I kept really busy for the next few days so I would not be consumed with the worry of what might happen. At about 6 o'clock on the Wednesday night, the phone rang and I was very surprised to learn that the caller was Bishop Michael Malone.

Bishop Michael asked me how I was and I told him that I'd been better. He said that he could understand my feelings as John had told him about Daniel's allegations against Father Jim Fletcher. I was stunned that John had told him and immediately felt very uneasy. The whole matter was in the hands of the police and I was perplexed and angry that John had mentioned it to the bishop. Of course he worked closely with the bishop and I guess he just wanted him to know. He wouldn't have had any idea of the repercussions of such a disclosure and the importance of the bishop's subsequent actions on the whole investigation. Bishop Michael said that firstly he wanted to convey his sympathy for the pain that I was no doubt experiencing and that he was offering help for whatever I needed through the difficult and perhaps long time ahead.

He said that John had told him the day before (Tuesday 4th June) about Daniel's visit to the police and that he had been up to see Father Jim that very afternoon (5th June). I held my breath and felt my chest pounding and then asked him what Father Jim had said. The bishop said that of course he denied he had anything to answer for and was understandably very upset. I said to the bishop that of course he would deny any allegations, to which Michael Malone replied, "For what I know of paedophiles, they lie through their teeth when confronted." He said it was very important to believe Daniel and that it was my and John's roles as parents to do so.

The breach of trust that we had experienced from Fletcher as a religious person probably fuelled my disappointment and anger at the bishop and I asked him why he had gone anywhere near Fletcher. He said it was to offer pastoral support to a brother priest. I told him indignantly that if Fletcher didn't know he was being investigated then he didn't need any support. At that stage I saw the visit as a 'tip-off' and resolved there and then to inform the police of the bishop's visit to Fletcher.

The bishop told me that he had "put Jim in touch with Fathers Burston, Harrigan and Saunders to support him through this time." He then said that from that point on, he would be "stepping back and waiting" adding that "people were innocent until proven guilty."

He then offered any support the church could provide in the way of counselling and said he would be back in touch. I told him that I would need help as John and I had exhausted each other worrying about Daniel and it was difficult now we were separated. I told him of the pain of seeing a son struggle with some aspects of his life and how proud I was of him for being courageous enough to put up his hand. He said he would ring me in a day or so and help me with whatever I had decided regarding counselling.

I decided not to tell Daniel that the bishop had been up to see Fletcher as I knew he would be upset. He was coping with enough pain from the Church as he unravelled the tightly-bound secret he had protected for years. I also assumed rightly or wrongly that he would be very disappointed and feel betrayed by the knowledge that his father had spoken to the bishop. John's motives weren't sinister and we all, at that stage, were still trying to trust the Catholic Church.

Daniel had told me that Detective Sergeant Peter Fox, whom he had met on the previous Monday, was a decent man who had reassured him that a fair investigation would take place. I thought about the bishop's visit to Fletcher and then the repercussions of such a visit dawned on me. I find it hard even now to accept that it was anything other than a tip-off.

I knew Fletcher had inappropriate literature in his possession as he had tried to hand it around at a dinner party that he'd held at the presbytery years before. John and I were having dinner with him and three other parishioners, laughing and talking, when he fetched a manila folder from his room and said for us to look at his latest collection of funny pictures. Naively, I leant over only to see a sketch of a fisherman standing in the water with a fish nibbling his penis. I didn't read the caption and I didn't think it was funny. Too surprised to say much more than, "Yuk, I don't want to see that," I stood up and went into the kitchen to start the washing up. John also left the table and Fletcher called out to us that I was to make sure I didn't see any penises out there either.

I was embarrassed and insulted and perhaps should have left the dishes for the other laughing guests, who were splitting their sides looking at the rest of the sheets in the folder. I felt like storming out but I didn't. We finished the dishes and then left. Fletcher knew he had upset me because he apologised later. I've enjoyed plenty of risqué jokes in my life but not from a priest. Handing around smutty pages at your own dinner table is very poor form, I think. My immediate thought was that, because of the bishop's warning, Fletcher would have disposed of any inappropriate material.

I also knew Fletcher's reaction to criticism of any kind and knew he would be protesting his innocence, shoring up support for himself and generally character assassinating our family, given the chance. Now he had just been given that chance by his own Church under the guise of a visit of pastoral care from the bishop.

I rang Maitland Police Station on the Friday and asked to speak with Detective Fox. I was told he was on leave for a few days and asked whether anyone else could help. After being passed on to three more people and eventually leaving a message with the last one, I was told someone would get back to me.

Detective Fox rang me from his holiday on the Saturday morning. I did understand that Daniel's visit to see him the previous Monday was very confidential but I wanted him to know of my concern that Fletcher had been tipped off. He was understandably furious and said that one of the important factors in an investigation was the initial confrontation with the alleged offender and the observation of how he reacted. The element of surprise was a legitimate investigative tool. No longer a tool in this case! He also said that he hoped the bishop had a good memory for he would surely find himself in the witness box. He said no doubt he would meet Daniel's family as the matter progressed and he asked me to write down, to the best of my memory, the full content of the bishop's phone call on the previous Wednesday.

The bishop rang back the next week to put me in touch with a counsellor. I was well supported by this person for the next three years and probably was kept sane through the whole traumatic saga. Despite my grievances with the bishop, the counselling was a very positive offer from him which I have greatly appreciated. When I finished my visits with that person I thought I was at peace but the ongoing repercussions of the damage to my son, my family and the extended family of friends as well, still affects my life very significantly and I often struggle with the grief. Loss of family relationships and loss of trust in Church are obstacles too large to climb over very often. Christmas has just passed and talk turns to church and attending so often. Again, I was told quietly by some people that they had either given up or refused to go because of what happened to Daniel and in particular by the Church's perceived responses at the time of the police involvement.

One day during this time, I was visiting my mother, aged eighty-eight, at her residence which was in a Catholic Aged Care community down by Lake Macquarie, when I noticed Bishop Malone's predecessor, retired Bishop Leo Clarke walking in the sun. We knew him quite well and had socialised with him on many occasions in the course of John's employment. He lived in a self care unit in the same complex as my mother and I stopped to say hello to him. He asked about my health since my marriage break up and then about my troubled son. I made a quick decision to tell him about the investigation into Fletcher. Standing in the morning sun, I gave him a brief overview of Daniel's disclosure and the subsequent police investigation. I had no idea of whether he already knew but he surprised me by saying

"Well Father Jim was always a bit of a worry. He always went home to mummy for a roast lunch on his day off and never socialised or played golf with his fellow priests. He used to drive us crazy at Bishop's House with all those young fellows hanging around eating us out of food and he made a big man of himself swearing and smoking in front of the boys. His jokes left a lot to be desired in a priest."

I was stunned at his reaction and thought about it later. In a way, he had recognised some aspects of the profile of a paedophile and had applied them to Fletcher very readily. Surely it's reasonable to wonder why the hierarchy of the Catholic Church hadn't initiated checks and balances to monitor such a man who exhibited such telling behaviour.

13

We were now in the second half of 2002. Daniel began to give his statement to the police and we held our breath again as he struggled with the trauma of remembrance. Later on we were made aware that Daniel would sit with Peter Fox and give his statement for a while but when it became clear to Peter that Daniel was emotionally exhausted he would cease the recollections and leave the process, going back to the police station a few days later. We learned that the priest started to abuse Daniel when he was a little boy in Year 7 and the abuse continued for about five years. There were over eighty occasions of offences in that time and we were further overwhelmed with the pain of the knowledge. He was working in a very busy environment and found it difficult to be with the police for a few hours and then go back to work and be the motivated people person he was supposed to be in that particular job. His staff management skills were well developed and he was more comfortable being the leader rather than a reliant person.

It must have been very hard for him at this time. The months rolled by and he would occasionally talk in general terms of the abuse and his statement. I was shattered to learn that he was still at a very preliminary stage of the process after a few months. As mentioned before, I knew the priest would be busy talking about his innocence. I finally met Detective Peter Fox and he assured me the whole thing was progressing but given the nature of the allegations it was not unusual for the length of time being taken. We were worried about Daniel's depression and stress levels and he gave me his guarantee that I could call him night or day if I needed help. That was a great relief.

Many people who saw Daniel struggling with anger and alcohol abuse didn't know the cause. As the months went by, more people learned the story. Some of them were told by the priest's friends and others by Daniel himself in the grip of upset. I don't suppose any of Fletcher's supporters actually questioned why Daniel was exhibiting such signs of distress. Certainly as Daniel's depression worsened and he was hospitalized, more people found out the cause. The overwhelming reaction from people who were made aware of the trauma he had been subjected to, and was experiencing then, was that it explained the way Daniel had been living his life since leaving school. Every single person offered love and support and no judgement which was a rather telling reaction and may have been a comfort to Daniel if he had known. We were in a very difficult position as to whether we should convey the positive feelings to Daniel and that would alert him to the knowledge that people knew of the abuse or to keep silent.

Time edged forward. The last half of 2002 will forever be remembered by me and surely most of the family as being incredibly difficult. I think we were holding our breath and wondering just what was happening to us as upset followed upset, pain after pain. My dearest friend of forty years, Sharyn, lost her battle with cancer. I cannot write in this genre about her bravery and our pain. A wonderful person whose friendship and love still raises me up and will forever.

My home was burgled and precious items were stolen. Not worth anything at all on the street market but of immeasurable sentimental value to me. You cannot replace with insurance your deceased father's watch or the photos of your sick friend on her last visit to your home. These photos were still in the camera which was taken. I collapsed at work and was hospitalised for a week's bed rest which probably gave me some strength to cope with Sharyn's death, late in November, my mother's stroke in December and the unrelenting pressure of the investigation into the priest.

The one bright and joyful event of that time was the birth of Daniel's little son. It felt so good to have something to celebrate and I can tell you he was and is a most joyful little fellow.

I cried very bitter tears on that New Year's Eve as we counted down the minutes to midnight at my caravan where I always find peace and where I have run to many times to escape from the pressure of the situation. The next morning the red wine stains on the back of my sister's good white shirt were a puzzle as we soaked, it until I had a memory flash of me crying on her shoulder with a glass of wine in my hand. She has forgiven me! Daniel arrived for a visit on New Year's Day and we rejoiced in the ten-day-old baby and hoped that the year would be better. Wrong!

As the weeks went by, we could see a pattern to the struggles of Daniel. He would spend hours with the police and then come home exhausted and upset. His statement was taking considerable time to give because it involved details of his whole association with Fletcher from the initial meeting, the grooming period and then the years of abuse. Daniel was very drained and needed to go slow with breaks to recover. He was having counselling arranged by the police and he said at the time it was helping him to just get through his days. He suffered from a post traumatic stress disorder and was hospitalised for a time for his own safety. That was difficult for him and his partner and the little children. They certainly couldn't understand what was the matter with their daddy. I started to give my statement to the police in February and then had an understanding of the time it was taking Daniel to complete his.

As the time for me to begin talking to the police approached, I decided to talk to Daniel. We had respected his privacy and had not broached the subject of what was covered in his statement to the police. I had to steel myself not to ask about details such as when he had met the priest or how the abuse had evolved. However, I needed to hear something from him to help me face the reality of the whole story. We sat quietly one afternoon on a couch at home and I asked him if he could tell me anything that he felt would help me get a grip on the situation. He sat for a while, then looked at me directly. He was struggling to commence speaking and I said for him not to worry about trying to explain anything. He then surprised me by saying the words

"The St. Christopher medal. He (Fletcher) had one stuck on the dash board of his car to keep him safe while driving. I used to wonder what would happen if the medal could talk and tell someone what was going on in his car."

I knew that medal and Fletcher had referred to it once when I drove him in his car to concelebrate a funeral in Sydney. He jerked his thumb towards it and said "That little fellow will keep us safe!"

Enough! More than enough!

On the day I was to start giving my statement to the police I drove slowly towards Maitland, trying to stay calm so that my words would be coherent. I had left myself plenty of time for the half hour drive but as I approached Maitland, I began to get upset. Memories of the priest's involvement in my family began to bubble around in my head and so I pulled into a little park located about ten minutes from the town centre. I was actually physically sick. I was alone. I remembered the meals

I'd cooked for him, zucchini pie was his favourite, and the buttons I'd sown on his black shirts. Exchanges of Christmas and birthday gifts and dinner parties for his mother and sister and social gatherings with other friends of his were past memories that crowded into my thoughts. Dozens of snippets of conversations I had had with him were also recalled and I remembered the times we had asked him for advice when we were worried about Daniel.

What monster could reassure us that all teenage boys started to seek independence and break away from the family mould when he was the cause of Daniel's confusion and depression? A paedophile could. Those worrying incidents from the past when Daniel went missing and then the time his clothes went missing had taken on a sinister importance and I knew that my good memory, which the boys and my husband had often teased me about, would be an asset this time.

I drank some water, called on my wonderful deceased dad who had a fierce sense of fairness, to guide me, invoked St. Christopher himself to walk with me and resumed my journey. My statement took about thirteen hours over a few appointments. I believe Daniel's took over fifty odd hours. Poor, poor boy.

14

By now, knowledge of the investigation was shared with others as Daniel confided in some people in his upset, and as the priest's cronies quietly protested their friend's innocence. Much was made of Daniel's alcohol abuse, emotional instability and work changes. Obviously, these caring pastoral people hadn't been educated about the effects of sexual abuse on a victim's life. I hope they now have a clearer understanding so they just may be able to help the next victim who crosses their paths.

During this time Father James Fletcher was still playing an active role as Parish Priest of Branxton. Even though the Bishop knew of the allegations against Fletcher and had been advised by the police to remove him from his workplace and away from contact with children, he chose not to. In addition he had actually increased Fletcher's power base by giving him Lochinvar Parish to look after as well. The Bishop's lack of understanding about paedophilia being aligned to power and not to physical strength was worrying to say the least.

In his pastoral letter just after Fletcher's arrest, the Bishop wrote that he had sought advice from the NSW Professional Standards Office, and had sought clarity about the risk potential of the priest as per NSW Child Protection Legislation. He then said that he decided to leave Father Fletcher in place, "aware also of his poor health and near fatal stroke a few years ago." I and many others could not understand his reasoning. If Fletcher's health was so poor, then what was he doing servicing two parishes, country ones at that, where a fair amount of driving was required anyway?

The Bishop has learned and accepted much since then about the reporting protocols and I expect he will do things differently in the future. The Church's own professional guidelines were basic but adequate and if adhered to, would have made our journey more bearable. However, the Bishop shouldn't have had to learn about pastoral care. Surely that is an expectation in the Church and we didn't see much of it all throughout our horrible struggle.

In my discussions with Detective Fox I realised that he was very frustrated that the priest was still in his parish. He wondered if he was confined to the presbytery. I decided to phone the Catholic School at Branxton to ask about enrolling my children at the school. I was lying of course and did not have any primary age children. I asked if there were any priests in the parish and I was assured that Father Fletcher was indeed in residence and was regularly at the school visiting the children and interacting with them on the playground as well. Detective Fox was very interested to learn that Fletcher seemed to be enjoying a rather close association with the children of his parish. I did hear later, but not from this school source, that he also had an infants' reading group. The thought of that still makes me shudder.

I believe a formal complaint was made by Detective Fox at this stage to the office of the NSW Ombudsman. I have never been able to ascertain what transpired but I do know pressure was put on the Bishop to get him out of the parish and away from children immediately. Then and only then, was he removed. The parish bulletin of the time states that Father Fletcher was on sick leave and prayers were asked for him. No prayers were asked for my son. That was in March, 2003.

It was in this period that Daniel completed his statement, from his hospital bed. During the course of the investigation he had been hospitalized twice as the stress of his situation had caused him to become depressed and desperate. His doctor watched over him compassionately and respectfully and we were all very grateful to her for her kindness and professionalism. Daniel's family supported him as well and we were also comforted by the visits from Detective Fox and his assisting police officer. They were able to give my son a vision of the future when all the stress and pain would recede. Daniel was taken to various locations where assaults were alleged to have happened and photos were taken. How stressful that must have been for him. His father and I and

Daniel's counsellor went to Maitland Police Station on the morning his statement was completed. We sat in the police staffroom, in the strangest of atmospheres.

We met our son's counsellor for the first time and with confidentiality issues hanging between us, we both thanked her for looking after Daniel and she told us we had an amazing son. She left to go and support Daniel while he signed his statement and John put his head down on the table and cried. I was emotional too but it was overridden by relief that we had got to a point of some conclusion. John told me it had just hit him and that he had believed Daniel but at that point it had really sunk in.

Police officers in and out of that lunch room were all cheerful, supportive and those in the know were very respectful of Daniel. We smiled when we were offered coffee for the eleventh time. We did drink a few. We asked Detective Fox what we could expect to happen next and were told that they would now be working towards interviewing Fletcher. I can't speak for the rest of the family but I know I was apprehensive about that because of the time that had elapsed since Daniel had first approached the police and I knew Fletcher would have been well prepared for the coming interview. No surprises for him. I think Daniel went back to the hospital for another night.

I had also completed my statement by then and I know that the other family members all took their turns in that chair. The coffee bill at the police station must be considerable. There would have been a lot of police work in the following

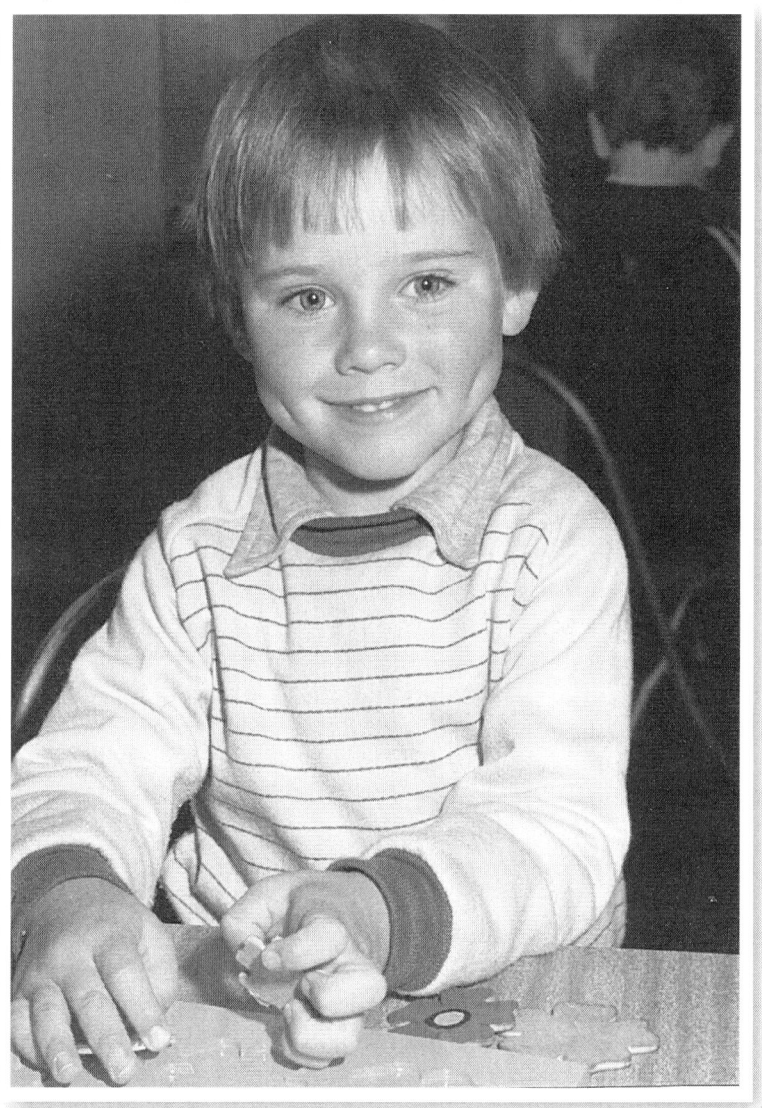

Daniel aged 4 years old.

Happy childhood. *Left to right*, Dominic, Luke, Bernard and Daniel.

Happy holiday. Daniel, Bernard, Dom, Pat and Luke in front of Dog on Tuckerbox.

Daniel being holy and happy on his First Communion day.

John and boys in those cricket whites.

James
Patrick
Fletcher

Bishop Leo Clarke and *Left to right*,
Luke, Bernard, Dom, and Daniel.

Daniel as a cadet, aged 14 years old.

Pat's First Communion.

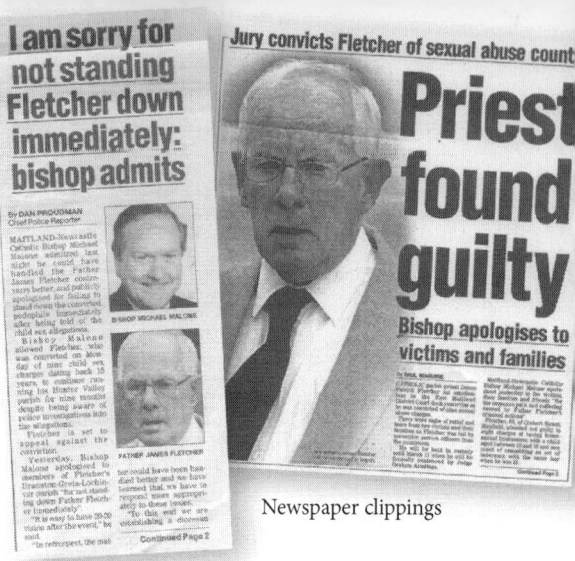

Newspaper clippings

Book launch for 'Holy Hell', 6th December, 2012 at the Catholic Cathedral Complex in Newcastle, NSW. Amongst the 250-strong crowd in attendance was Bishop William Wright (Bishop of Maitland diocese) and Vicar General Maitland Diocese, Brian Mascord. The launch was a resounding success, Pat's speech was met by a standing ovation and tears of appreciation from family, friends, victim support groups and the general public.

Next stop, another book launch, 14th December, this time at NSW Parliament House!

Photos from top left clockwise: The Feenan boys launching the book. Pat signing copies. Daniel, Pat and Peter Fox.

weeks of which I know nothing but we were told by Detective Sergeant Fox that the priest had been asked to come to Maitland Police Station at 9.30 on the morning of the 14th of May. I had dinner with Daniel and his family on the night of the 13th and we talked quietly about the imminent arrest of Fletcher. Many, many emotions were encountered that night and it was futile to try and sleep. In the dawn I realised that my main hope was for the legal system not to let us down because the Catholic Church had when it failed so badly in its duty of care to my whole family.

Of course Fletcher turned up with a solicitor and support clergy. Remember, he had had eleven months to prepare for this very visit, courtesy of the tip off from Bishop Malone. There was no search warrant executed on his presbytery as any damning material would have long been destroyed. He was formally arrested and charged with nine counts of sexual abuse against our son. It was explained to us that although there were numerous occasions of abuse, the Police and DPP (Director of Public Prosecutions) had settled on nine strong charges.

We were further upset to have our suspicions confirmed and learn that one of the charges related to the night of my father-in-law's birthday. Fletcher had arranged to meet our son at the end of a street near the birthday party and he drove him to a vacant block of land and abused him. We were shattered to learn that the egotistical priest had chosen Fletcher St in Adamstown for his disgusting pleasure. What monster could calmly face us at mass the next morning and reassure us that Daniel was a typical teenager wanting only to stretch his wings.

Fletcher was bailed to appear at Newcastle Local Court on the 25th of July.

Interestingly, he denied knowing our family very well and said we were just people in the parish. He must have forgotten about my role as member and then Chairperson of his Parish council for about five years, my husband's work on his Finance Committee and the four boys' roles as altar servers. I asked Peter Fox if he would like the photos of him attending dinners at our home and my fortieth birthday and also a stack of birthday cards from him. He was delighted to have them.

The media! The combination of a well known and local Catholic priest having alleged sexual assault charges against him and the fact of him obviously being left in the parish during the course of the investigation was too good a story opportunity to be ignored by the media. The arrest was a big swallow for some of us as we prepared for the next phase and with the benefit of hindsight we really didn't have a clue of how traumatic it was going to be. But really, who would? The headlines blared, the reporters busied themselves and it wasn't long before the Bishop found himself very defensive about his own role. A few people patted me on the arm in crowds and I realised that somehow they knew the victim's identity. Conversely, some people ignored us or hurriedly looked away in shopping centres and refused to make eye contact and we realised they also knew. I'm not sure whether they looked away in embarrassment or disbelief. I can't explain the emotions or motives of the man from Dungog parish who ran his supermarket trolley into me but I commenced wearing sunglasses when in crowded places from that day.

It wasn't long before the Diocesan rumour mill activated itself and stories and versions started to circulate. Newcastle is a particularly insular place and long time residents would acknowledge that numerous associations through school, tertiary education, parishes, sport and workplaces mean that Novocastrians constantly meet and reconnect. One may not know the person sitting beside himself or herself at a dinner party but it doesn't take long to establish a connection of knowing the same friends or people. Therefore the setting and players of this particular story were talked about in all manner of places. We heard some ghastly rumours and were upset often.

The anonymous phone calls were unsettling and I realised that if the priest's supporters had my phone number, then they automatically had my address. I had many sleepless nights. It must have been very difficult for my husband as he worked in the Catholic Church environment. He told me that many people avoided him and others took great pains to avoid any mention of his sons, any of them. However, he did have a few loyal and supportive priests to talk to but only a few of the sixty or so in the diocese were brave enough to extend to him the offer of support. Very priestly wouldn't you say.

We were particularly sad to hear that prayers were asked for Father Jim at Branxton parish. I certainly didn't mind if people wanted to pray for him and I privately thought that he would need heaps of prayers to endure the legal process ahead but there was no mention of prayers for the alleged victim, my son. Surely he deserved the same courtesy and pastoral support as the accused priest? I believe one brave priest eventually tried to address this very issue and suffered the consequence of breaking ranks.

I was told later that the prayers for the priest still happened, they had just gone underground. I can say that the family of James Fletcher were in my own thoughts and prayers at this time. I acknowledge that they loved their son, brother and uncle and they would have been very upset I'm sure. I don't know if they felt my prayers or if they prayed for us. I didn't blame them if they in fact hated our family.

When the dust settled after the arrest, I decided to contact the Catholic Church's Professional Standards office. I was still worried about the Bishop's intervention and I recognised that I was struggling myself with the horror of the knowledge of the abuse against Daniel.

I wrote that I wished to make an allegation of emotional and spiritual abuse and of mental shock and cruelty by Father Fletcher to myself. I wrote of my desolation and loneliness for the church and my dismay when I learned that a priest who celebrated mass in my home, who purported to be a spiritual adviser to my family and who had encouraged me to play such an active role in my church community was a criminal of the worst kind. The local diocesan community were not supportive so I thought that the Church, through their Towards Healing program might be able to help me.

Wrong! The reply from the Director of Professional Standards dated the 16 th of June, 2003, was disappointing and depressing and furthered my developing view that the church did not want to know about this troubled family. The Director wrote: "I write this letter to confirm my telephone advice of 5 June 2003 that your statement of complaint is not caught within Towards Healing, given that the definition of Emotional/Psychological abuse is only applicable to such abuse occasioned directly to a child victim." He had told me in the phone conversation that my complaint was not captured by the guidelines of their organisation and I asked him to put it in writing. For Christ's sake this was my beloved son and their guidelines were cowardly.

I made an undertaking to myself that when the legal proceedings were over, I would write and protest and write and agitate and write and convince until the bloody guidelines were changed to include the families of victims. The recognition by the church of the enormous damage done to families by the abuse, the knowledge of the abuse and the terrible breach of trust was and is very important to me.

15

Our first time at Court was memorable. We arrived together and stood about outside on the footpath. One of the boys spied Fletcher up the street but on the other side. He was wearing huge dark glasses. I had not seen him for a few years and had an overwhelming desire to go and confront him. The two policemen with us warned me to keep my distance and ignore him. I know that Daniel's two brothers who were with us, wanted to knock him to the ground, at the very least. Same warning to them. A busy Courthouse verandah is not such a pleasant place and we began to feel uneasy as people surged around us exhibiting varying degrees of temperament. A little room was found for us and we crowded in. Daniel and Donna, his fiancée, talked quietly in the corner and we were warned not to talk about anything pertaining to the charges. We had noticed one of Fletcher's mates, a minister from another denomination church, smoking near us earlier so we heeded the instruction.

There was a rustle of activity and the New South Wales Director of Public Prosecutions lawyer and officers went by wheeling a large suitcase. A lot of statements had been taken and along with items gathered, this paperwork formed the brief of evidence to be presented to the Court. We were invited to enter the court room's ante chamber and had to go through a checkpoint. There, manning the scanner, was a lady we had known many years before. She asked in a very friendly fashion about the boys and what they were all doing now and I think I just looked at her stupidly. Surely they have tact classes in Court personnel training. There we were with three of the aforementioned boys and she was rabbiting on about them.

Once inside, we were confronted, at fairly close range, by Fletcher's supporters. We knew most of them and that hurt. Daniel was particularly upset to see the parents of a girl he had been very friendly with at school and of course they just stared at us. Fletcher's friend, Father Des Harrigan was also there and he avoided contact as well. Father Jim Saunders ushered Fletcher through and into the court room and then came and sat between the two camps. He did greet us and I silently thanked him for his fairness and priestliness.

We were all invited in to the courtroom and in a very rapid process heard Fletcher plead Not Guilty to the charges. Another court date was set and we drove to a quiet place for lunch together. Daniel's support person, a very old friend with a happy and positive personality was a decided asset that day.

Up until this plea of Not Guilty, we had all nurtured the

hope that the priest would plead guilty and that of course would save Daniel from the daunting experience of being the chief prosecution witness in a criminal trial. That was not to be however and so we embarked on a long process of Hearings, Adjournments, and Appearances.

The year dragged on and Christmas came and went. By this time, Daniel had decided to give up work and was in fact unable to work. We were finally given a date for a trial. It was to be the 31st of May, 2004 at East Maitland Courthouse. This old building is sited on a hill, surrounded by Jacaranda trees and is quite picturesque but is dominated by Maitland Gaol which is just across the road. Our family had all driven by it many times, never imagining we would be one day having such horrible business there. We now had something definite to work towards. Family members arranged holidays and work schedules. I guess we were all walking on egg shells with Daniel and doing a lot of counting down. Daniel, understandably, wasn't sleeping well and I know the stress was beginning to mount for the rest of us. Our lives were certainly on hold as we prepared for a dreadful experience.

On the 26th of April I received a phone call at work from Detective Fox. He had rung me there on numerous occasions during his investigations and I was well supported by my boss as he allowed me to take the calls and then gave me time out if I was upset. We had agreed, with Daniel's permission, that I would field the phone calls from the police and the DPP as Daniel was understandably often upset by them. The idea was for me to gauge Daniel's emotional state and composure and choose the appropriate time to discuss the latest development with him. On this occasion, Detective Fox told me he had something to tell me and asked if I was I sitting down.

He told me that there had been a major development in his investigation and that another alleged victim of Fletcher had come forward. I remember saying "Thank Christ!" That was going to be a large help in Daniel's quest for justice, but I certainly had regrets for the pain of another victim. All along, the police suspected that Fletcher was so complete a paedophile that there had to be other victims out there. All the police could tell me was that this latest victim was older than Daniel and that he didn't know Daniel at all. I asked what would happen as the trial was only five weeks away and he told me that he couldn't say at that stage but it may have an effect on the trial date. He did say that this was a very important development and could only help the Prosecution's case.

Relieved would be an apt description of the reaction of Daniel's father when I phoned him immediately after the police call. We believed the knowledge of a new victim would take some of the pressure off our family and perhaps convince the non believers of the truth of the charges the priest was facing. I rang Daniel and asked if he could call in on his way home as I had something to tell him. I can still clearly remember the look on his face when I told him that there was another victim.

He looked at me and quietly said that now people would believe him. We both talked about the effect it might have on the trial date and of course we wondered about the identity of the other person. I remembered that Daniel had told me that Fletcher didn't know it was him ringing on the night of that Sixty Minutes program and I now realised that there was another possibility as far as the priest was concerned. He left to go home and then I held my breath. I realised that Daniel was pleased about the new development but I feared that when he thought about it, he would be very hurt. He still had mixed feelings about the priest. Sure enough, by the next night he had considered the bigger picture and he became very upset. He rang for help and I wasn't surprised to hear him say that through the whole assault time frame he thought and had been told that he was very special to the priest. Now he realised that he was just 'the next one on the list!'

Daniel's brothers were shocked about the new developments as they considered the ramifications of the priest's predatory behaviour. They all realised that he had indeed targeted their beloved elder brother. My son who was living in Canberra became very upset. I had one long night with him on the phone and he was very drunk and very emotional. He told me that he had always believed Daniel's allegations but somehow the knowledge of another person's pain had 'cemented the story' for him. As he was about five hours away, I was in a bit of a dilemma about how to help him. All mothers would understand my anxiety. When that child calls for help, we swing into mother bear mode.

Luckily, I remembered a school friend who lived in Canberra and luckier still, she was home when I rang her.

What a good friend she was to have listened to my hasty story and offered to help straight away. She arranged to see Dominic in the next few hours and with one of her own sons accompanying her, took Dominic to lunch, calmed him and arranged a visit to a lovely young Catholic priest. Strange remedy some may say, but he was a great man who acknowledged the pain caused to Dom's family by the paedophile priest and apologised. It is strange to reflect on a complete stranger apologising to our family, when the Maitland Newcastle Catholic diocese was not able to offer any solace or even prayers to help us through that enormous distress. Calming words, a good night's sleep and he was a whole lot better.

16

Daniel settled down and listened to the advice and instructions from the police and the DPP. They believed their case against Fletcher would be strengthened if they could include the statement of evidence from the next victim which Peter Fox had completed. Apparently the Defence has to have all the evidence from the Prosecution a certain time before a trial and in this case, there wasn't enough time to include it. Therefore, they applied to have the trial date vacated. They also had explained before, that Fletcher's trial had not been given a Priority One status and there was a strong chance that the trial may not have proceeded on the 31st of May anyway. We were all very disappointed but did accept that a later date might give a better chance for a better outcome.

Because of our inexperience with the law we were very appreciative of the several opportunities we were given to become acquainted with the Crown's desire to establish tendency and similarity evidence by using the new victim's statement. If his evidence could be allowed to be heard during the trial, it would demonstrate that Fletcher had the preponderance to prey on and molest small boys even before he had met Daniel. From what I did know of the law, I had the opinion that a victim could be disadvantaged by it. An accused person could be on trial for an offence and have a long history of similar charges, even imprisonment. The jury, as the law stood then, were unable to be told of those previous offences so as not to disadvantage the accused and to ensure he or she had a fair trial. Proclivity could not be established and cases were often very difficult to prove without it.

After discussing my concerns, about the length of time the whole process was taking, with officers from the DPP and the Police, I decided to write to the Director of Public Prosecutions and the Attorney General. I explained my concerns about the toll it was taking on the family and of course Daniel in particular, and asked that a new trial date be set with a Priority One status. I felt strongly that we were all desperate to get it over and done with before another Christmas and we wanted to try and resume some sort of normal lives. What relief we would experience if a New Year dawned and the muck was over! I did receive very courteous replies and was told that correct protocols were being observed by the various departments.

The Attorney General wrote and informed me with the following:

"…Director of Public Prosecutions assures me that his officers are doing everything they can to deal with the matter as quickly as possible. However, the interests of fairness require the court to be satisfied that both the prosecution and defence have adequate time to prepare their cases. Thus, when new evidence is presented that strengthens the case of the prosecution, the court allows the defence time to respond to it. Otherwise, there is a chance that decisions may be reversed on appeal."

Good news cheered us in the next few weeks. The second victim was prepared to attend court if needed and then a third victim came forward. This man was sixteen years older than Daniel, and as before, we were not able to know his identity but we were told that he didn't know our family.

Unbelievably Fletcher had also approached that family for character references. The audacity of this man! A pattern was certainly becoming evident about this particular paedophile priest and such arrogance beggared belief.

I think it was around this time that we were told that one priest from a neighbouring parish had used part of the previous year's Christmas collection to help fund Fletcher's defence. I was disgusted as I thought of the many people who attend church at Christmas and only Christmas for their very own reasons.

Perhaps people who had known pain and suffering in the past year or who had been disillusioned in some way had decided to attend church in the season of peace and goodwill. They may have hoped that a fresh start could be made with the celebration of Christ's own birth. And then, in a spirit of generosity fuelled by their new found peacefulness and joy, they gave happily to the Christmas collection thinking it would go towards a very worthwhile cause, and then it was diverted to the legal fund for a paedophile priest! They'd never darken a church door again if they knew and I would understand completely if the regulars ceased attending as well. We were later to learn that the priest using donations for Fletcher had at one time also faced child sexual abuse charges.

That was the Christmas that Daniel's depression had rendered him incapable of organising any funds to provide a Christmas celebration for his family and I and a few friends bought and paid for it all, with love, unconditional love. Soon after that, the diocese, through the Bishop, started to support Daniel financially and that was appreciated and took a weight from his shoulders. I know that Fletcher had been offered money for the legal fees for the defence of the charges. I was told that Bishop Malone had asked who was paying Daniel's legal fees and perhaps he was thinking of helping with them, but he obviously didn't understand the legal process and didn't realise that this was a criminal matter being prosecuted by the state and not by the Feenan family.

Daniel was in close contact with Detective Fox throughout this hiatus as well as the DPP. All officers extended to him the utmost patience as they dealt with his very understandable frustration. They discussed the various possible outcomes of the criminal trial with him and us and we were warned that the result is not always what a victim hopes for. I was present with Daniel on one occasion when he was asked what he hoped for from the whole legal procedure. He answered readily that he fervently wished that the priest would admit to the abuse and say he was sorry. Daniel didn't care if Fletcher went to gaol or not and said that it was not the purpose of all of the investigation. No malicious intent there, just that little boy inside wanting confirmation and apology. What courage and character typified that statement. There weren't many dry eyes in the room after that.

Finally, a new trial date was set and it was to begin on Monday, the 23rd of November, again at East Maitland Courthouse. We were told that it had been given a Priority One classification so with no significant unforseen circumstances, there was a strong chance it would proceed as set down. What a relief! A look at the calendar confirmed that we had a major family wedding the week before and we wondered if that would be a happy distraction.

The weeks crawled by and the stress of the wait again took its toll on Daniel and Donna. Holidays were again applied for and that special sort of leave that you suppose you will never need to access was granted, without question. A new round of subpoenas was issued and we started to prepare again.

The DPP told us that Fletcher's defence being spearheaded by Ian Barker QC, a prominent lawyer from Sydney. He was the man who, as Solicitor General of the Northern Territory, many years before, had successfully prosecuted Lindy Chamberlain for murdering her daughter, Azaria. I was told that he was the man who got the dingo off and I wondered about the similarity between the dingo and the priest, both predators. He got it wrong with that case and I hoped he'd have no success in the priest's trial.

He didn't come cheap either, but somehow the funds were pouring in for Fletcher.

17

I talked to Daniel about support for him at the trial. He had previously asked an old family friend to be with him, a man who had been present for some of Daniel's bad episodes of anger and upset and he had agreed. Our family and close friends had all suggested that support might be one way of helping us all through what promised to be a very difficult period but they were naturally very mindful of Daniel's feelings. Obviously there was going to be some very sensitive material mentioned at the trial and no one wanted to cause Daniel any more pain. I conveyed all of the offers to Daniel and he said he would think about it.

When I pressed him for an answer so people could arrange time off from work, he told me he thought he would like them to attend. He was understandably embarrassed and I reassured him that the people who loved him were offering love and support and it was entirely his call whether he had them in the waiting room at the trial or in the actual Courtroom itself. He asked me to tell all of those family and friends that he would like them there but he would wait until the time of the actual trial to see how he felt about having them in the Courtroom.

A few weeks before the trial was to commence, Detective Peter Fox suggested that whoever was available might like to go to the Courthouse and get a feeling for the actual Courtroom itself. We were grateful for the understanding that we were shown and realised that the suggestion was a good one. We were absolutely resolute in our determination to hold our heads high and pursue justice so anything that would help prepare us for the ordeal ahead was welcome. Daniel, Donna, Bernard and I drove over and met him and the solicitor from the DPP at the East Maitland Court House.

They showed us where the different court personnel would be sitting, where the jury would be and most importantly where the accused would be sitting in the dock. It was helpful to visualise him sitting there and we hoped it would lessen the pain of seeing him at the actual trial. Detective Fox showed us the room which had been allocated to Daniel and his supporters and the room he supposed the Defence would be using. We were able to sit in the witness box and orient ourselves to the court scene, judge to the right, priest and legal teams to the left.

I thought it was a worthwhile visit and two and a half weeks later when I found myself entering the crowded courtroom, I was certain it had been a brilliant idea. I was still anxious but not shocked and Daniel said that it had been a tremendous help to him and he would not have liked to have gone in there without the prior introductory visit.

The wedding of my niece a week before the trial was a grand affair. She was getting married from my home as her parents lived seven hours away near Moree. We threw ourselves into the wedding preparations which gave me the most pleasant anticipation, joy and distraction. Without a daughter of my own, I had no idea about the hair styling, makeup, massages and general delight that happens on the wedding eve and morn. It was a fantastic experience.

The wedding eve dinner was a very friendly affair as we met old friends and relatives and it was a joy to see the cousins rejoicing in each other's company. Of course they all knew what was going to happen in a week's time and indeed the next day, but when the ten of them are together, they become like the little children who devoured those plates of sandwiches, rode bikes at breakneck speeds around the paddocks and played in the creek until dark. They laughed and joked and celebrated when my third son, Dominic surprised us all by arriving at the venue from Canberra. He was meant to come the next day so he was very well received.

I looked at all those beautiful young people and became very calm. I knew the wedding would go well but I had a moment of clarity of thought and could see that we would get through the coming weeks because of the love and strength of the family.

The wedding did go well. My elder sister, the mother of the bride, had spoken quietly to the Catholic officiating priest and he was sensitive to the undercurrents running through the church on that day. My niece was gorgeous and her proud husband was both happy and handsome. It was indeed an elegant and happy occasion. In keeping with the honesty of this story, I must own up to a night which had a rather blurred ending for me. I know that the young 'uns wanted mum and aunty to have a good night because she had been under rather a lot of stress, so they all made sure her glass was topped up. Big headache the next day, some confusion on my part whether dessert had been served at all but probably the best medicine an anxious mum could have had. It makes for great family recounts when the kids are together and there is only the slightest of hints of my condition on the wonderful DVD that a great brother in law produced and a loyal and precious god daughter edited.

18

Wedding over, Trial next.

We tried to have a normal week but that didn't happen. The countdown was on and we were counting. Messages of support flowed to all the family, some I could relay to Daniel, some I couldn't because he didn't know that those particular people knew of the assault charges. We were told by the police and DPP that there would be nothing much happening for the first day while the legal arguments were happening and then the jury empanelled. The legal argument is when the Crown or Prosecution, us in this case, and the Defence, argue in front of the trial judge about what is admissible as evidence. This includes witnesses and their statements.

On the first morning of the trial, Monday, the 22nd of November, 2004, I woke very early and immediately thought of Dan. Had he been able to sleep and was he okay? The thought of the immediate future for my family caused me to feel ill and in fact I was physically sick. Even though the day was something we had anticipated for a very long time, I still experienced the incredulous feeling that we were even in such a situation. As I write this, I remember the pounding chest, the headache and the stomach upset. A calming cup of tea sipped out near my rose garden, a read of a little prayer a friend had given me (strange thing that) and a good long stare at my father's photo, him being the champion of fairness and justice, helped me to settle and regain my equilibrium.

I had resolved not to contact Daniel and Donna and just meet them at the Courthouse but he rang about a minor matter concerning the kids. He sounded strong and straight away I lost my nervousness and in fact got off the phone and said "Bring it on!" If Dan could do it, then he could depend on his mum to walk with him, beside him, in front of him or wherever he wanted me to be.

The arrival at the Courthouse was memorable. We knew that on that day, we probably would not be required as witnesses, but nonetheless we needed to be there to make a start and show our resolve. As our family's cars pulled in and parked, along with those of supporting friends, we gathered together. Everyone kissed everyone else and then Daniel and Donna arrived and everyone then kissed them.

As a group we walked towards the court house and people standing around watched. I know they were saying "which one is he?" and some were insensitive enough to point. As the boys look fairly similar, they may have had their work cut out to pinpoint which one of the four was the victim. I am so proud of my four sons for the way in which they conducted themselves that morning, quiet, straight and proud. We stood about near the steps and Detective Sergeant Peter Fox welcomed Daniel and his entourage. The media, the priest's supporters and court staff milled round until the doors opened. There were quite a number of people gathering around an entrance on the other side of the courthouse and I assumed they were potential jurors. We were ushered into a little room which was to be ours for the duration of the trial. We stayed in it most of the time but did step out for fresh air now and again and of course the smokers left it often. The priest and his friends were allocated a room as far away from us as was possible and given that the Courthouse at East Maitland is not large, that was quite an achievement.

A Court officer pointed out that when the trial actually started, there would be witnesses in the next room, through a locked door and we would not be able to see or speak to them until all had taken the stand. We knew then that he was speaking about the other alleged victim who was still unknown to us.

On that first day, we sat about in our room, talking quietly until lunchtime. We were told that the trial in relation to witnesses taking the stand, would not commence that day or even the next day in all probability. We left, had lunch nearby and went our separate ways. I remember Luke came out home to have a swim and Daniel and Donna went to pick up their children and then they came home for a swim as well. We were all fairly quiet but the boys enjoy being together and the afternoon passed.

The next day, Tuesday, found us back at Court. We sat about again and talked. I had packed sandwiches and I think we realised that food would be needed over the next few weeks as we would be spending many hours sitting around. Detective Fox said the DPP liaison officer would bring a kettle and tea and coffee each day. My family, cousins and nieces decided to take care of the catering for the dozen or so people who would be with us each day.

From then on, eskies arrived each day with sandwiches, cold drinks and something sweet. After the trial was over, I remember the senior Court officer saying he had never, ever, seen the likes of such hospitality during a trial. He agreed that it was obviously the way that support could be offered to Daniel by people who were not going to be able to testify.

We were told, by the DPP that afternoon, who was allowed to take the witness stand and in which order we would be called. The legal arguments had been completed and ruled on and many witnesses for the Crown had been disallowed. Victim three had been ruled out because the nature of his abuse was different and there had been too much time between his abuse and Daniel's. We were dismayed that so many people had been excluded and hoped that the Prosecution had enough left to make a compelling case against Fletcher. Another trip home and we were worried about this latest development.

Wednesday, and there we were again. We sat in the room while the jury was selected and empanelled. Two jurors who had been excused because they knew us went by the door. One fellow briefly put his head in the door and cried. He was very upset, had not had an idea what matter he had been called up for and was shocked. He promised to pray and went on his way. Finally it started.

Up until that afternoon, family and friends had offered support by being with Daniel and us at the trial, but were not sure about actually sitting in the courtroom and hearing the evidence. Because they were good friends and devoted family they already knew of the pain experienced by Daniel and respected him and his decision about their presence while he was actually in the witness box. Perhaps the time sitting around with people as we waited for it all to begin had helped Daniel and he said he didn't mind who came in and in fact he would welcome the support.

A last kiss, a hug and away they went leaving John and I and our other three sons in the green room. We could not be present as three of us were witnesses and two were on standby in case they needed to be called. I remember holding Daniel's hands and saying that he had waited a long, long, time for what was about to happen and I would be willing him to display the strength, courage and self respect that I believed he had. We told him we loved him, were proud of him and to hold his head high. As soon as he walked through the courtroom door we all cried. I was very glad he had aunties and cousins in there but that need to protect Daniel on that day was overwhelming and when we couldn't, then, get a hand on him we were numb and lost.

That is the hardest parting moment I have ever had, even worse than the day my husband walked out the door. Daniel was certainly bathed in family and friends' love but as his mother, I felt the pain of separation because for the purpose of the criminal trial, my son was going back to when he was a little, innocent boy in danger and there would not be a mother in the world who would not want to be with her child at that moment.

I walked outside and sat on a seat on the verandah. Beneath the hilltop Courthouse, is a view of East Maitland. I could see ordinary daily activities taking place and people going about their usual routines without knowing and most probably not caring about the events on the hill. I guess you would be immune to drama if you lived next door to such a place. A young mother with a stroller and a little boy walked towards the railway line and I had an irresistible urge to go and talk to her. I wanted to be back where she was. A train rattled by and I wondered about the passengers idly looking out the windows. It seemed strange that they could not somehow see what was happening up on the hill. Rail travellers are anonymous witnesses to the blur of humanity they glimpse as the trains rushes by and the buildings just become part of the speeding landscapes.

19

Inside the court room, the trial of James Patrick Fletcher had indeed begun. It was the 24th of November. The Prosecution and Defence had stated their positions. Daniel was put in the witness box. He was gently led through his story by the Crown Prosecutor. I have been told by all the people who were in there that day that Daniel was quiet, unshakeable and very credible as he retold his terrible story and explained his experiences. The DPP witness liaison officer came out of the courtroom to tell us that Daniel was doing well and that there would probably be a break in about half an hour for lunch. More crying but this time with relief that Daniel was able to answer and speak without fear. I know John and I started to open the eskies of sandwiches and soft drinks that my niece, the darling who had been married just over a week before, had so thoughtfully packed.

Footsteps were heard up and down the corridor and the doors opened. People began spilling out and I could see that they were nearly all in tears and then Daniel came out. There was an awkward moment while supporters breathed deeply and shuffled. Good girl Aunty Paula, my beloved cousin who strode over to Daniel hugged him and said

"Well Daniel that was really awful but now do you want an egg and lettuce sandwich or meat and tomato?"

There was a collective sigh of relief and then instant chatter. Daniel said to Paula that he would love the egg but first he was going outside for a smoke. At that moment, the whole room full of family and friends were uniformly very glad that Daniel was a smoker. One health conscious aunty said

"Daniel why don't you have two!"

We were very mindful of the warning that we, as witnesses, had been given from Detective Fox. We were not to discuss Daniel's evidence with him or one another. People milled around and told us Daniel was courageous and we all chatted in a strangely relaxed way over lunch. That is not the only time that Paula's sense of humour and quick grasp of a situation, relieved the tension in those few weeks.

The trial resumed. Inside a room next to ours, another family waited also. Some of their family sat in the court room and some stayed with the other alleged victim of the priest who would be giving evidence some time in the next few days. I wondered who they were. We shared a kettle with them and Detective Fox or the DPP officer went between the two rooms as we were to have no contact with them. At one stage, we heard them talking excitedly and there was laughing and exclamations. We were told by a policeman that a daughter had arrived unexpectedly from overseas and they were all joyous. I knew exactly how that mother was feeling. We did offer some of our food to them, via Detective Fox, and they in turn had someone called Aunty Shirley who cooked for them and also brought in cakes and a sample of her Christmas pudding for us. I was starting to get an inkling that this other family did things just like ours.

The media started to make eye contact with us. Previously it had been heads down and talking to one another as they filed past. The cameras were outside as well and we tried to ignore them and we knew that they could snap off whatever they liked but they would be in contempt of court if they tried to publish any identifying photos.

Another break was called and this time our people were angry. They had watched and listened as the Defence's fancy and very expensive QC had tried to discredit Daniel's evidence. People were incensed as he tried to trip Daniel up on his evidence. Barrister Ian Barker QC put it to Daniel that he let Father Fletcher have sex with him again and again without opposition. Daniel replied that Fletcher had made threats and that's why he did not say anything. Barker tried to get Daniel to admit that he had made the story up so he could get money and Daniel said he had not.

"Do you think I would put my whole family through this?" he responded.

Peter Fox had warned they would probably take this tack. That is the best explanation defence can come up with when a priest is alleged to have committed sexual assault.

There was further confusion as photos of a site near Paterson were looked at. Daniel kept his cool as a pile of photos were passed to him to identify.

I have not spoken much about the specific acts my son endured. They were just as upsetting then as they remain to this day. Daniel had never been able to talk to me about the specifics of what happened. He had said that it was just too painful. Instead he asked me to read the statement he had made over many painful hours to Detective Peter Fox. I remember reading the statement and breaking down time and again as well as being physically sick. It was a few years before I could read it completely. I felt compelled to share my son's pain as I didn't share it at the time of the abuse because I wasn't aware of it.

I have wrestled as to whether to include any detail of any of the acts of abuse. It still brings so much hurt but I don't believe I can convey the full gravity of these crimes without reference to the acts this pitiful excuse for a priest, this vile predator, perpetrated on my beloved son. It will shock and revolt, but I have decided to include reference to 'one' of these crimes, only one of many my son was subjected to over the years.

I have edited substantive portions I consider too graphic and invite you to skip the following section if you find it too distressing. I ask you to share my pain and remember my son was only fourteen years of age when this happened.

He turned into the park on the right side
of the road as you head into town. Being
after lunch on a Wednesday there was no
one about and he drove down a dirt road to
where there is a heavy planting of trees, I
think they were Poplars or something like
that. He drove the car into the middle of all
these trees and it would have been difficult
for anyone going past to see us. I was
expecting to have to give him a head job but
he then said to me "You haven't orgasmed.
How would you like to orgasm? It feels
great."

(6 lines deleted)

I could tell that he was starting to
become annoyed and angry with this. I felt
very uncomfortable. I felt that it would be
something that I would enjoy from what he
told me. I discovered that I didn't like it at
all. I didn't want to say this to him because
he was becoming angry anyway because he
couldn't give me an erection. I said, "It's no
good it won't go hard. It's uncomfortable.
It's hurting. It's not going to go hard." He
then sat up a little annoyed and said, "Okay.

I know what we can do. I know another way
to make you orgasm." I said, "How?" He said
"have sex." I said "How do we do that?" I
really didn't know what he meant. I knew
men and women had sex together but I
couldn't understand what he was suggesting
by the two of us having sex. He then said,
"Okay what I will do is

(4 lines deleted)

I had heard about homosexuals but I
didn't understand that having sex like that
was what homosexuals did. I just didn't know
about these sorts of things. Like the oral sex,
I just accepted whatever Father Fletcher
told me and if he said this is what you do to
orgasm I just accepted this was alright, it
was normal.

(18 lines deleted)

This continued the pain but I didn't cry
out. I was crying, tears were running down
my face. The pain inside me was unbelievable
but I couldn't move, I couldn't cry out. I was
in so much pain that I laid across the seat
with both my hands clenched. I remember
my knuckles being white and he was just

(1 line deleted)

For some silly reason I looked up and again I just focused on that bloody silly St Christopher's Medal he had hanging near the steering wheel. It was as if I just focused on that it would take all the pain away and make me forget what was happening but it didn't.

(13 lines deleted)

I was sobbing and he could see the tears running down my face and the pain I was in. He just hugged me and cuddled me into him.

(8 lines deleted)

He told me, "That's your first one and you will have more from now on." It was really weird. Just like a parent congratulating a kid for scoring a goal in a sports game or something like that. He could see I was still in terrible pain and crying but he said nothing about this. I then bent down and pulled my pants up and he then started to tidy himself up and fix his manner of dress. I then sat back in the car. He went around and got in the driver's side. He then lit up a cigarette and had a smoke before he drove off. I was still sobbing and he said, "Are you alright?" I said, "It's still hurting a bit." He said, "That's okay. It's only natural, it will stop."

He then drove to a small shop in Paterson and bought a can of coke. He didn't buy two, just one for both of us to share. He turned around and drove into town and let me out near the school. All the way back from Paterson he just kept on to me about this being our secret. He kept saying "No one else is to know about this. It is great you have had your first orgasm."

(3 lines deleted)

He kept emphasising more than usual that this was a secret and I was to tell no one about it.

What you have just read is not only a parent's worst nightmare but so much more. The pain of that stays with me always and I have no hope that it will ever leave me. I know Daniel carries it with him forever.

These details were so horrid that one DPP solicitor broke down after reading Daniel's statement and asked to be taken off the case which was upsetting to hear as those solicitors are so used to reading sexual assault briefs.

Eventually, Daniel was let stand down from the witness box. He had acquitted himself to the best of his ability. He had courageously waded through a mire of the most disgusting abuse descriptions and a fairly predictable, but upsetting, cross examination.

He had been checked about a date and period of time from his youth when he had said in his police statement that he missed some school because of glandular fever and alleged abuse had happened then. In our own bloody home for goodness sake! The school roll was produced and the absences marked didn't support what Dan had said. Daniel was asked if he could explain that and he said he couldn't, he just remembered being sick.

I could have explained it. The symptoms of glandular fever with swollen neck glands, very sore throat, and fatigue and fevers were very similar to what he experienced with chronic tonsillitis and it's no wonder he may have been confused about the nature of the illness that had caused him to miss school after one lot of holidays and miss it he did. I remember the priest himself came to the house once to anoint Daniel with the Blessing of the Sick because he was so debilitated with one of these illnesses. It's bizarre and sad at the same time that a priest cannot remember performing this Sacrament but I do think he may have remembered coming to bless Daniel in the Intensive Care ward at the John Hunter Hospital after Dan had sustained a serious head injury after a fall.

Daniel told me one day that when he woke up after the brain surgery and saw Fletcher standing beside his bed he thought he had died and gone to hell.

20

Daniel was escorted from the courtroom and I was then called to give evidence and led in to the Courtroom by a court officer. I sat in the witness box and took a very deep breath, looked at the jury members and saw that they were ordinary men and women and surely that meant that they would be able to recognise that our family was an ordinary one as well. No obvious religious members sat amongst them as far as I could determine. This had concerned me as I was aware that the jury was drawn from the local community and Maitland had traditionally been a stronghold of the Catholic Church. The diocese of the Hunter Valley had been known as the Maitland Diocese from its inception in 1847 until 1995 when the name was changed to the Maitland Newcastle Catholic Diocese.

I took a long look at Fletcher in the dock. He had his head down and would not meet my gaze. Perhaps that was just as well as I may have been unwise enough to shout at him. He knew that I now knew him for what he was, a criminal of the worst kind. He would remember those conversations I had had with him about my worries about Daniel and his false reassurances that all boys became secretive in their teenage years. The sight of the mother of the victim leaping into the dock with hands reaching for his neck would have given the legal tables a shake up. No. Two and a half years of dedicated police work could not be wasted.

I did agree that Daniel was my eldest son, born at the Mater Hospital and I did agree that I understood what he had alleged had happened to him at the hands of our friend, now ex-friend, Father James Patrick Fletcher. I confirmed some of the circumstances of the times when Daniel had said he was abused. The gentle questioning by the Prosecution was welcome as I was feeling very nervous and strained. I was asked to leave the Court room while a matter was discussed and I never did find out what it involved. Daniel was in the green room when I went in and we had time for a hug and a cry before I was recalled. Daniel had to wait outside in case he was needed to give further evidence.

When I went back in, it was time for my cross examination. I was asked to look at Daniel's enrolment forms for St. Peter's and note that I had given the name of a friend, who had older sons at the school, as a contact person and there was reference to her son as a person with whom Daniel was acquainted. I agreed that I had trusted the woman at the time and that was in 1989. Up until that moment, there had been no sign of that particular family but I knew they were very staunch supporters of Fletcher. He was their friend and they had enjoyed a long association with them. They have five sons. I knew they had been very kind to Mrs. Fletcher, the priest's aged mother. You see, they had been our friends too and our photo albums are sprinkled with memories of social occasions we enjoyed with them and Fletcher and his family. The husband was the Confirmation sponsor of one of our sons and I can clearly recall telling that lady I was worried about Daniel and the change in his personality as a teenager.

In that instant, I could see what Barker was trying to establish. If the mother of the victim trusted this woman, then that woman could be regarded as a reliable witness. Of course she was a reliable witness and I knew she had integrity but all the supporters of Fletcher were victims as well. They did not want to believe such terrible things about their friend. I said once to a non believer who rang to harass me that if all the people in the world who didn't want to believe the accusations were lined up, then you would find John and Pat at the head of the line as we definitely did not want this to be true. However, we knew, as surely as we knew that the sun was going to rise each day, that we were hearing the truth from our beloved son.

I was also able to tell the court that Daniel had suffered a very serious bout of Glandular Fever one Christmas. I remember saying that Daniel had missed Christmas because of it. The judge asked me to explain my statement and I qualified it by saying that Daniel struggled out of bed to look at his presents and then collapsed into his bed for the rest of the day and also the next. He missed Christmas. I was told that I had finished and was allowed to sit in the court room. Warm smiles of encouragement from family and friends helped me settle as much as I could in the circumstances.

John was ushered in next. I watched him as he swore on the bible as I had done and wondered if Daniel had also done that. He was also led through a series of identifying statements and then he got the question that I would have liked.

"Can you describe the relationship between your family and the accused?" he was asked.

We all leaned forward willing John to say that the boys were excited every time the priest called in, to say that he always bought presents for the boys, and to say that Fletcher took a very special interest in Daniel. He may have been able to mention the meals cooked, the buttons sewed on priestly shirts or the friendship that had developed between my mother and the priest's mother. John didn't get these details out but did mention that the boys liked Fletcher to call in. He could have mentioned, if given the chance, that when we went on holidays, touring around the eastern states, the boys always spent their pocket money on buying bloody souvenir spoons for Fletcher. He never had too many, he just bought more spoon racks to display them.

He was also asked about the missing bag of Daniel's clothes and I thought how wily Barker was as mothers' know of such details, not busy dads. John was asked how he would have known that the clothes were Daniel's and he mentioned the school logo. A keen mum knows where the repairs and tears are on the uniforms that she launders every day and could probably recognise items in a clothing pool. Those missing clothes had become very important. On one of the occasions of abuse, Daniel had changed into his shop clothes when he was with Fletcher and then the priest had dropped him at his place of work. The school clothes were inadvertently left in the priest's car and because it was the last week of the school year, there were no more chances for Fletcher to see Daniel secretly. An innocent man would have casually dropped that bag at home and said that Daniel left it behind after an innocent lift home from Maitland. Instead, the clothes "turned up at school" early the next year when Fletcher resumed his evil actions.

Afterwards, John was very angry with himself for not being able to describe the relationship between Fletcher and his sons. He actually said that he thought that he had let the family down and we glumly agreed.

I had sadness for him as I know how difficult the whole process had been for him. It's bloody hard sitting in that box and only being able to answer specific questions. Aunty Paula to the rescue again! Just before John left the stand, Ian Barker leaned over to him and said something which we didn't catch. Later my sister asked John what he had said and Paula quipped that he had asked John if he would do his tax. Laughs all round and I think John felt better.

When Luke was called in next, John and I were sitting together in the court room. We sat together for the rest of the trial and I was certainly comforted by his presence and I guess it showed solidarity from us given these dreadful circumstances. Luke waved away the bible and took the alternate oath. Luke was able to tell the court that he and his brothers thought that Fletcher was a top sort of bloke and he did mention the sweets the priest always had in his car. Of course alarm bells never rang for us in the past. Perhaps if he had worn a trench coat instead of the clerical collar, we would have had serious thoughts about the lollies and about the way he encouraged the adulation of the kids. No, he wore the garb of a demure catholic priest.

Into the court room, out of the court room, we trooped as a group and as instructed. John discovered his mobile phone had been stolen during one of the sessions and he was very indignant. After a few startled comments we realised we were in a court house and there were dishonest people about. It was a bit of a jolt to remember that, as I suppose we thought people were like ourselves, innocent victims caught up in matters beyond their control.

The next witness for the Prosecution was an ex neighbour of ours. He was able to testify that Daniel was indeed out and about one night in Glen Oak when he was about fifteen years old. He told the Court that Daniel looked upset when confronted by one of his guests at a party and that Daniel said he had been out chasing his dog which had run off. That night was the occasion of one of the specific charges when Daniel had met the priest at the river near our home. He had told the court, I learned later, that he had to stand on his 'tippy toes" while Fletcher had anal intercourse with him. A true and gut wrenching statement from a young boy's memory. All the way through this terrible account, my son used the language of a little boy when describing his ordeal. In the retelling of his experience, he became that little altar boy once more.

It was the weekend. We all scattered and tried to have a couple of days of normality but it was hard to get off the merry-go-round and be ordinary. I think the boys sought each other's company and had a rather quiet few days. If they didn't, they were kind enough not to tell me. I know I went to my cousin's to sleep as I didn't want to be alone. Monday morning saw us all back at the Courthouse and into the green room.

It was Detective Fox's turn in the witness box. I watched and heard him give calm and clear answers to the questions he was asked. He gave details of his investigation into the alleged paedophilia charges and I reflected, not for the first time, how lucky we were to have had this professional man in charge of our son's painful story. Our friend in the legal fraternity knew Peter Fox was the right man.

We were shown a video interview taken at the time of the priest's arrest. In the legal argument at the commencement of the trial, the length had been reduced and edited from three hours to about forty five minutes. In the interview, Fletcher said he had never done anything of a sexual nature.

He said "My religious education was if you did sexual things, you died and went to hell. I never did sexual things because of that fear."

He went on to declare "No one has touched me or sucked my penis or done things of a sexual nature to me. Never."

I was interested in the interview because I knew that he was not going to take the stand himself and this would be the jury's only chance to see him declaring his innocence. The jury didn't know that the Bishop had told him of the allegations eleven months before his arrest and he had used that time to prepare himself for such an interview. They didn't know that he had asserted that he hardly knew the victim's family and yet I had photos of him sitting up at my fortieth birthday party, his mother and my mother chatting at home one night and numerous other photos and birthday cards which proved our relationship went further than the one he may have had with a random person who cleaned the church brass. I hoped that his reference to Daniel as Danny at the end of the tape would indicate to the jury members that he had indeed had an association with my son.

Bearing in mind that the original sites of the abuse could have changed significantly in fourteen years, it was suggested that the jury be put in a bus and taken to the sites to see the environments for themselves and to clear up any misunderstandings of just where the trees were that Daniel had described. He had said that Fletcher had driven into Tucker Park at Paterson and parked behind some trees. I believe the jury got the general picture when they were on site.

Later I heard that the Defence were taking photos in Paterson Park from the wrong angle. Luckily they were spotted by Detective Fox who was able to tell them that those photos, if printed, would give an incorrect perspective to the members of the jury. I am sure that the priest's friends and legal team were indeed grateful to this man as they surely would not want to have misrepresented the evidence.

Throughout the time that I had been allowed to sit in the Courtroom and listen to the witnesses, I was aware of strangers sitting there as well. I wasn't sure who they were and wondered about their interest in the case. Detective Fox told us that some family members of the one victim who was allowed to testify, were present. He also said that a third victim, whose evidence had been excluded from the trial, was attending.

There were also several people, who were obviously supporting Fletcher, sitting in the court room throughout each day. I say obviously because we all had to share a bathroom and early on after I gave my evidence, I found myself in the toilet area with a tall red-headed stranger whom I had seen at the Newcastle Court sitting with Fletcher's friends and in the car park of the East Maitland Courthouse. It was a bit awkward and our eye contact was minimal until she knocked me into the wall of the bathroom as she turned around and then whirled out. I was shocked. I came out rubbing my head and explained to the family what had happened. I declined to take any action wanting to believe it was an accident. A good woman of the Church would not stoop so low as to assault the mother of the victim, surely.

When we assembled again in the Courtroom, there was

a change in supporters. New faces were there and I noticed a lady who had 'grieving and distraught mother' written all over her face. We knew the next witness was another victim of Fletcher's and he had said that he didn't mind if we sat in and heard his statement. This was conveyed to us by the DPP liaison officer. Detective Fox had said that we may be upset when we first saw him. I wondered if that was because we may have known him despite what we had been told and that was that we didn't know him and he did not know us personally.

We sat waiting for him to be called. I watched. The door opened and a young man was escorted into the Courtroom and up to the witness stand. I know my jaw dropped. I felt it. The man on the stand could have been Daniel's twin. Same height, same good looks and colouring and the same bearing. There was a ripple of movement from the supporters, the jury and the press gallery as people turned to look at Daniel and I know they would have been noting the resemblance between the two victims. Daniel and I exchanged a look of clarity. I know he could see himself up there in that box and this had been what Peter Fox had tried to warn me of.

That brave victim was led through his statements by the Prosecution. It must have been hard for him to say the words with his parents and siblings listening to every word. His evidence was graphic as he told of being a thirteen-year-old altar boy who had twice stayed alone with the priest at his presbytery. He alleged the priest came in to say goodnight to him and had performed oral sex on him. This was repeated about a year later on another visit. He was asked not to tell anyone. The man kept his secret for seventeen years and told no-one until Fletcher had asked a member of his family for a character reference in relation to his defence in my son's matter. What arrogance on the part of this paedophile!

Ultimately this had prompted this second victim to break his silence. Ian Barker asked him if he had made up the story and he denied doing so. When asked if he would be seeking compensation, this young man replied that it was not his intention to do so. He did not claim Criminal Injuries Compensation, he did not claim compensation from the church and he was not planning to pursue his own allegations. This left the Defence with no motive for this victim's evidence other than he just wanted to tell the truth. He was a total stranger but a fellow victim of this cruel predator of a priest. We will be grateful to him forever. He left the stand and walked out of the Courtroom.

That was the conclusion of the Crown's case against Fletcher.

21

There was a very brief recess and then the Defence commenced its case.

The first witness called was the priest's mother. There were audible exclamations of disbelief from the gallery as she walked in. This poor woman was about eighty-eight years old at that time. My family had felt compassion for her throughout the long months since Daniel approached the police. I know for sure that she loved her son just as I loved mine. The Defence were trying to establish a pattern of behaviour for the priest and I know he did regularly visit his mother on Tuesdays. Some of the abuse occasions were alleged to have happened on his days off which were Tuesdays.

At one stage Mrs Fletcher was asked to leave the witness stand and to wait outside for a few minutes while something was discussed. She tripped as she stepped down and I suppose it was a rather telling moment when Daniel leapt to his feet to aid her. A court officer helped her and escorted her outside. The priest hung his head and I hoped he was suffering. No old lady should be put through that. I have no doubt that they used this poor old woman purely on the basis of a sympathy vote. How cruel.

When she was cross examined by the Prosecution I prayed (funny that) that she would not be upset but I needn't have worried as the Crown Prosecutor was very gentle with her. Without any goading at all, he led her to admit that

"Jimmy came for lunch and nearly always dinner on Tuesdays" but that was only when she was home and she did agree that she had some holidays and other engagements. The priest sometimes called in and had a pot luck tea with us after visiting his mother so he certainly didn't dine there every week.

Fletcher's very good friend and the lady I mentioned before as the contact person for Daniel at school was next. It was established that if Fletcher was needed by his parish on Tuesdays, he could be reached at his mother's. I don't believe anyone would have a problem with that as it was well known that Tuesday was a Jimmy day.

However, the next witness, her son, was harder to listen to. He talked about the difficulty of getting away from school without permission, names being checked on rolls and then checked off at the end of the sports' afternoons and then he made the extraordinary claim that the school was fenced. I guess the gasp from the Maitland locals present in the Court that day convinced the jury that he was mistaken in that particular claim. Anyone familiar with Maitland and St Peter's High school in those years, would know how easy it was to walk onto the river bank or up into the Heritage Mall. Dominic had in fact scored a detention from one such stroll to the river to play on the rope swing and to have a smoke. The Prosecution noted that the Defence witness was now a teacher and suggested that he may have been influenced in speaking about procedures by the nature of his present employment rather than recollections as a student. I believe he acknowledged the possibility of that.

Daniel later said that he didn't attend much of the sport that had been discussed as he was very much involved with representative sport and he was coming and going from school a lot in relation to that.

The penis doctor was next. He gave a lengthy and professional opinion on the priest's penis. There were photos and explanations of irregularities and at the end of his testimony there was a very loud silence. I'm not sure what the doctor proved but it was necessary for the Defence apparently because Daniel had stated that the priest's penis looked partially uncircumcised, whatever that meant, when in fact the paedophile owned a penis that had been circumcised. I don't think Daniel was an expert at thirteen years old, with his limited observations of his family's and friends' disparate models. The priest would have been very embarrassed, the media reported that he cried and I wished that he'd kept it where it belonged and none of this would have happened. Ultimately the issue did not add to or detract from either case.

That was the conclusion of the Defence case for the accused Catholic priest, Father James Patrick Fletcher.

We left the courtroom that day, a scorching, smoky day of overcast sky and searing westerly winds and made our way down to the cars. The family of the other victim walked in front of us and we slowed. Even though we had been told that after both boys had given their evidence we no longer had to be segregated, we had had no opportunity to make contact. As we neared the cars, we tentatively moved together and I can remember finding myself in the arms of the other mother and we sobbed on each other's shoulders and then spoke of our brave and each other's brave sons. We introduced ourselves to one another and our families and friends and I can truly say it was another significant moment of my life. What a courageous son they had to come forward and put himself through all of that, just to support a perfect stranger. He is in my heart.

As we all milled around, Daniel started to drive away when he spotted the other victim who had been slower coming down to the cars. Daniel stopped and they hugged each other through the open window of the car. What they said to each other I do not know but I do know there was not a dry eye in that car park. I looked up and saw Detective Fox standing under a tree nearby. He had his handkerchief out and I don't think it was for the bushfire smoke or perspiration. These lovely people were not strangers anymore and were to walk the path ahead with us. I knew the door would be open between the rooms now. Another round of hugs and we all headed away to escape the heat and onlookers.

Sitting at home that night, I had time to reflect about the other family and the shock that they must have been experiencing. They had not had a long time to prepare themselves for the devastating allegations their son had made against the priest and they had found themselves embroiled in a sordid and painful event and in the public spotlight where many people had an opinion.

I spoke to Daniel and he too was thinking of them, especially the other victim. I know that in the ensuing weeks and months the two victims spoke regularly and they found a degree of comfort in doing that. They were both stunned and indignant to discover that they were not so special to the priest after all. The full realisation that they were the victims of a complete paedophile weighed heavily and they both suffered.

Another victim who was prepared to testify against the priest sat through every day of the trial. He also would have been reflecting on the evilness of the accused. The priest had actually been charged with this older victim's matter and we were waiting to learn the outcome of that arrest. This man was older than my son and the other victim but we could all see that he had the same good looks and eye colouring as the younger fellows and we could recognise the pattern of preference of the priest.

How many blue/green eyed former Catholic altar boys of Fletcher are out there hiding the secret?

22

The next day saw us arriving at the Courthouse with a different feeling. We knew there would be no more evidence from either side and we had been told that the summing up would proceed. By now the media interest in the case had increased and we walked through onlookers and media representatives as we made our way up the stairs. I know we all felt relieved and comforted that no identifying information could be published but I was also feeling alarmed about what would happen at the end of the trial in relation to publicity.

Into the green room and for the first time, the con-necting door was open and we could speak to the other family. We didn't have a lot to say to them as words didn't seem enough but I know that we had formed a bond the day before and it didn't need any words at all. We all shared the bond of being victims of this evil priest. My happy cousin, who had been sick the day before, was back and as usual, I felt her comforting presence. Our loyal family and close friends who attended the Trial day after day were amazing. They gave their time, hospitality, warmth, compassion and most of all their love, daily, and without it, we would have been desolate. Food arrived on my doorstep, flowers and kind words as well and gestures such as these, made an enormous difference to me as I realised the extent of the silent support our family had.

Not having been through a criminal trial before, in fact not any trial, I was completely unprepared for the day of summations. The Crown Prosecutor summed up the Crown's case against Fletcher. I had not heard any of Daniel's evidence and so I was very upset to hear it as presented again by the Crown. I learned that my son had been groomed by James Patrick Fletcher for the purpose of sex and of the extremely painful experiences he suffered as a thirteen, fourteen, and fifteen-year-old "at the hands of a person who held great authority over him at the time."

The charges of eight counts of homosexual intercourse with a child aged between ten and eighteen and one count of committing an aggravated act of indecency with a child, were known to me but were in some part of my brain where I had hidden them and had not processed them very well. To hear those charges described in detail was very painful for me and to Daniel's father and brothers as well. Each charge was explained in full and the words "excruciating pain" and "anal intercourse" ripped aside any last vestiges of protection I had afforded myself. This was raw and real. I know I cried through most of that session and I know I was crying for Daniel, our family and for the future as well as the past. How could anyone recover from that? What if the jury didn't believe Fletcher was guilty and he was acquitted?

After raping my beloved son, the priest bought a single can of coke and offered Daniel a swig. Mundane little details like the selfish purchase of one can of coke helped a realistic recall of events by Daniel. At the river near our home, Daniel said he had to stand on "his tippy toes" during one session of abuse and that certainly evoked a distressing mental image of a helpless little boy suffering at the hands of a paedophile who had told him that their times together were special but who made threats to my son if he told anyone. The knowledge that he rode his bicycle home "standing on his pedals" was cruel and unequivocal. I personally have anguished now for years that Daniel was not able to tell me what was happening to him and I have had to reluctantly accept, along with all the other mothers of victims throughout the world, that paedophile power is evil but superior to parent power. Did Fletcher feel the force of my murderous feelings towards him at that time?

The Crown summed up by saying that the alleged victim's account of "such painful experiences was convincing and consistent." He also said that the minor details recounted by the victim gave truth to his account and that the evidence provided by the alleged victim's family members and a second man who alleged Father Fletcher had performed oral sex on him gave the Crown's case strength. He acknowledged the Defence's claim that no-one in their right mind would take such enormous risks to take a victim to a public place for sex but said it was not a question of whether the acts were "dangerous or foolhardy" but whether they had actually occurred.

He went on to say that "people do take risks, especially when sexual matters are involved, people do have sex in public places."

Of course in reply, Mr Barker QC tried to discredit the Crown witnesses. He disputed the Prosecution's view, saying that the alleged victim was "unlikely in the extreme to be telling the truth" and that he had made up deliberate lies and monstrous accusations. He again mentioned money as a motive for the accusations. I had learned earlier that when he actually put this supposition to Daniel when he was cross examining him, Daniel had said a very definite "no" and added the question

"Do you think I would put my whole family through this?" Barker also told the court that the priest would have had "a death wish" to engage in oral and anal sex with a young boy in public, especially when his personalised number plates "advertised" his presence. He mentioned the evidence of his Defence witnesses and concluded his summation.

This had all taken quite a few hours and we were all feeling a bit overloaded with words and emotions. For me, the mother, the grief at hearing the details of my boy's abuse was overwhelming and shocking. I stood about uncertainly as a feeling of numbness enveloped me and tried to think what I had to do next. In my heightened sense of motherhood, I had begun to feel responsible for everyone.

A close friend of mine, who is also my doctor, took one look at me and suggested that we might leave the Court House and find a quiet little spot for coffee. I guess she was wearing both her hats at that stage. The forty minute break was beneficial and I did try to relax but I know my mind was back at that bloody courthouse. We drove back and I know the family looked at me anxiously and at her gratefully. The normality of dispensing sandwiches and cups of tea had been very helpful to the supporters who stayed at the Courthouse. Mindless but welcome routines!

As we milled about outside, the press gallery spoke to us. No names were exchanged, although I realised they knew damn well who we were. I mentioned to one lady that it was nearly over and she said it would still be a while as the judge had to speak. She was right. I went to the bathroom and glanced into the Defence's room. I think I was wondering where Big Red was and would she elbow me again.

They were praying and I bet Daniel wasn't included in their prayers.

23

After noticing the praying supporters of the priest, it struck me again that throughout the whole trial, our family had not seen, in our room, one religious representative of the diocese or in fact the Catholic Church. I knew various priests had popped in "to wish Jim well" and assure him of support and one of these men has since told me that he didn't "like" to come near us in case it upset us. That has to be the all time weakest statement. We were already as upset as we could be and a visit may just have helped us cope. We, at the time, were a room full of Catholic people who had lived their faith well and at the time were emulating Christ himself by showing love and compassion to one another. We had with us through those dark days, four ex-school captains of Catholic secondary schools, my two sisters who were both Religious Education Co-Ordinators of their respective Catholic schools, numerous Ministers of the Eucharist and assorted Ministers of the Word,(readers at mass) plus church cleaners. We were a very Catholic flock but we lacked a shepherd.

We listened to the judge sum up the whole trial. Once again, I heard about the crimes against my son and the arguments for and against the alleged charges. Through a blur of tears and anger, I heard Daniel described by the judge as convincing, credible and courageous. Good enough. The instructions to the jury were long and complex and I hoped they were listening carefully. The judge finished speaking and the jury left to consider the case and their verdict. I gazed at them as they filed out of the courtroom and willed them to find justice for Daniel.

In our room, we waited. The police, DPP officers and supporters all said they hoped we had all done enough for a conviction. I was tortured with missed opportunities and perceived lack of clarity of some of the statements. Throughout the trial, I had sat at night writing notes to pass to the Prosecution team about some of the anomalies and they were very courteous as they read what I had written. I tried not to be tiresome and I know I don't possess a clever legal brain but I was the mother and felt disempowered.

What was plain to me became lost in legalese rebuttals even if I had made a valid point. What did reassure me was the statement from the DPP staff saying that they thought they were presenting a strong case and they did not want to muddy the waters with peripheral issues. They explained that Daniel had been an excellent witness, and of course I hadn't seen him in the witness box, and they were not worried at all about obscure dates and the likes.

I had written about similarities between Glandular fever and tonsillitis and I had quickly sourced the medical reports, which they had asked me to get, to prove that Dan had experienced symptoms of both conditions for a couple of years when he was a teenager. The reports were obtained because Daniel had asserted that he missed school one February after the holidays when he had Glandular fever and in the cross examination the school roll was produced and didn't support his statement. It certainly did later in the year when he had been absent after another lot of school holidays. I hoped a jury member would turn the pages and see these documented absences. Daniel said later that he just knew he was very sick with a swollen throat in one lot of school holidays and couldn't return to school.

We had an uneasy lunch and there was talk of how long the jury would be out. A sheriff explained to us that if the jury members had a question to ask the judge, then all court personnel had to go back into the court room and that included the priest. After nearly two hours we were told the jury had a question so in we all filed. I stared at the jury members' faces trying to see if there were any indications as to what they were thinking. One man glanced in our direction but he also looked at the priest.

The question that had brought us all back in to the court room was about the number of parishes Fletcher had been in. I believe it was something like

"Is it usual for Catholic priests to serve in so many parishes?"

I'm not sure if the jury received a helpful answer and I don't believe there was anyone in that courtroom qualified to venture an opinion on that. They all trooped out and we returned to our room. I remember saying to John and Detective Fox that I believed the jury was on the right track as they were thinking about the priest's past movements. Others weren't sure and disagreed.

Throughout the afternoon we were relieved that Daniel and some of the boys stopped smoking for a while and had a few games of cards. It was an interesting sight to see them sitting on the floor playing Euchre, a game which the boys had played every night in the caravan on our holidays. They could have been anywhere in the world. I reflected that Detective Peter Fox was a man for all seasons as he joined them for a couple of games and his supporting presence was much appreciated. At the end of the day and with still no word from the jury, we were told that we would be going home and that they would resume their deliberations the next day.

The DPP liaison officer packed up her cards and commented that they had been a great success and she would bring them the next day. She asked if there were any other games we could think of that we might like and trust Paula, she immediately asked for Twister. The room erupted with laughter and we had a mental image of all those men in suits twirling and twisting round each other. We left the Court House in a lighter mood and hoped that the next day would be our last one there.

Friday morning saw us back in the courthouse and I know we were all beginning to feel the tension of the last two weeks. Some official paperwork concerning witness expenses needed to be completed and that took a few hours. I hadn't realised that we would actually be given an allowance for attending and was surprised. I think I knew that members of a jury get paid but again with no witness experience, I hadn't given it a thought. I don't know what the others did with theirs, but I was more than happy to give mine to the Salvos for their Christmas Appeal. I'm absolutely positive that many of the people they help are past victims of abuse and perhaps they weren't lucky enough to have supportive family and dedicated police working with them to seek justice.

As we sat in our little room at the morning tea break we wondered about the jury. Cousin Paula said that if we had to come back on Monday, she would be bringing the Christmas tree to set up. We all laughed and then really started to worry about what the jury were thinking about. The DPP and police explained some of the scenarios if they weren't able to reach a verdict. They talked of mixed results, hung juries and the remote but dreadful possibility of another trial. Just as we were thinking about lunch, the court officer came to the door and told us the jury was coming back in. Instant anxiety.

As we found our seats once more in the court room, I noticed that Fletcher's supporters were looking jaded as well. I wasn't concerned about Fletcher as I believed and still do, that he could have made a terrible situation better by pleading guilty and sparing my son, our family and in fact his own family the distressing and very public trial. If they believed in him, I imagined they were traumatised by the whole process. They were victims also. The jury filed in and took their seats.

I had prepared myself for the revelation that they couldn't reach a verdict and held my breath as the judge read what they had written. Relief. They were requesting a copy of Judge Armitage's legal instructions contained within his summation given the day before. There was a long and protracted discussion about the best method of obtaining such a copy and plans were made to take the original to Newcastle, with a police escort, to ensure a secure copy was made. The technology was not available in Maitland and both sides agreed that the jury could not have the original in case it was damaged. The tape and its escort left and we all dispersed for lunch.

Over lunch, Dominic decided that he would probably go back to Canberra that night as it was looking as if there would be no conclusion. His employers were getting impatient and they were correct in saying that his official part was over. Later on that afternoon, at about 3.45pm, the oral tape arrived back at the East Maitland District Court and the jury returned to the court room half an hour later to request leave to continue their deliberations on the Monday. They were granted leave and so we faced another weekend of waiting.

It was three weeks until Christmas Eve and I think we all talked about making some sort of an effort to get organised for it. Perhaps some Santa shopping would help but I don't think any of us had the heart for it. Really, I believe we just scattered to our homes to start counting down the hours until Monday morning.

I travelled to Newcastle to attend a Christmas celebration with kind people who had invited me to share their night. I didn't know the other guests and I hoped that it would be a kind of escape but as Newcastle is a strange place where many people know many people, it wasn't long before connections were made. As we were sitting round talking of Christmas and the end of the year, a lovely lady, a perfect stranger to me, just started to talk about the trial and said she knew who the father of the victim was, not personally though, and it was tough on the whole family especially because he worked for the Catholic Church.

To speak or not to speak! I made a quick decision because I didn't want the lady to be embarrassed later if she found out my identity so when she reiterated that it was a terrible ordeal for the victim I agreed and said quietly that I was his mother. Silence. I assured her that I wasn't upset with her for speaking about it and in a way it improved my night as I had to lift myself to prove to her that she hadn't ruined mine and in the end that cheerfulness commandeered my numbness and I had a very enjoyable night.

The rest of the weekend crawled by. We compared notes and we had all mowed our lawns. Daniel and his family drove up to my caravan and had a break away from the phone and sitting on the beach at sunset is really good medicine. A couple of friends either dropped by or rang and somehow the hours slipped by.

Worrying doesn't help an outcome but we were all anxious. I know that Daniel said he didn't have the stamina to go through it all again if the jury couldn't decide and I agreed and said he could add the five of us to that as well.

Sunday night found me praying. I was feeling pretty bitter that we had faced the whole ordeal, still without any word from the religious of the diocese and I wondered why they had been unable to support us. The mother of one of the other victims, the one whom I had met the week before, was also struggling with the knowledge that her family had been deserted by the very priests who had been part of her life up until her son disclosed his abuse. There was one exception. One brave priest had run the gauntlet of the wrath of fellow priests and the hierarchy and strongly supported that family.

The other mother also found it hard to attend court and sit across from a nun who was the godmother of one of her children and who now had become a public supporter of the priest.

My darling old mother was nearly ninety-one and completely unaware of what was happening in her family as she slipped away from us with her dementia but I was comforted by the knowledge that she would never know how we had been let down by her beloved church. Remembering her simplicity and resilience helped me to find peace that night. My prayers worked because I did sleep and felt calm as I drifted off.

24

Monday morning. Monday the 6th of December, four years to the day since Daniel had disclosed to me that he had been sexually abused. I drove to Court wondering if it would be another significant day and when I arrived and saw our loyal supporters arriving also, I was again overcome with feelings of awe as their lives were obviously on hold as they supported Daniel. They are wonderfully strong people and I will never forget their faith in us.

Throughout the morning, I spoke with the other mother and learned more about her other children and the effect that their brother's disclosure had had on them and their trust in the church. We had similar stories and similar pain and both wondered what paths our futures might take at the end of the legal proceedings. We thought that we might be able to help one another as we were in a rather unique situation.

The morning dragged on and we had a coffee break. By then the media were talking freely to us and we trusted them not to print anything which might prejudice the case. They expressed amazement at the numbers of family and friends who had been present each day and acknowledged the difficulty of the days spent waiting.

I would like to mention the reporter for the Catholic diocesan newspaper who had the onerous job of reporting the days at court to the Bishop and who had the journalistic responsibility of writing fairly about the criminal trial. In the early days of the trial she appeared very aloof and we were sad as she had taught the boys at school and her manner exacerbated their feelings of being forsaken by the church. However, as the trial progressed we began to share a greeting or smile and the awkwardness abated. I'm sure she still maintained her neutrality but we were the better for the eye contact.

After it was all over, she apologised for her initial manner and I was happy to accept her apology. She said that in the beginning, she was reluctant to speak to anyone in case the legal process was disrupted and she also said that she had found herself in a complicated situation. I was moved by the beautiful letter she sent to me later and in particular the words "…it was a privilege to share, in a small way, in such a significant time in your family's life."

We resumed our vigil in the green room and marvelled at Bernard sleeping, again, curled up behind the door. He had been working night shifts throughout the trial and hadn't had enough sleep. He woke up and was just telling me that he wouldn't bother with lunch but would keep dozing when, with a brief knock at the door, the Judge's Associate entered and announced, "the jury will now take a one-hour lunch break."

25

The gallery was packed. People I had not seen before were crammed in behind us and against the walls. We watched as the accused was led in shuffling, head down and bent over and he took his seat. What was he thinking about? I was numb. I turned around and saw Luke sitting with his arm around Daniel and Donna was holding on to him as well. We stood as the judge came in and there wasn't a sound in that room even though it was filled to capacity. We sat down and held our breath.

In what seemed to be a very quick progression, the judge addressed the jury and asked if they had reached a decision. The forewoman of the jury stood and said that yes they had. I heard the collective sigh that comes after breath has been held.

The judge's advocate immediately read out the first charge and asked her how the jury found the accused and she said,

GUILTY.

There was an audible gasp and the sound of sobs. I now know the sobs were mine.

The second charge was read and she again said

GUILTY.

I glanced round at Daniel and saw that Luke had encircled him with both his arms and I know I really started to cry then.

The third charge,

GUILTY.

The fourth,

GUILTY.

By then I was only listening for the rape charge.

GUILTY.

The whole nine charges.

GUILTY.

My head was nearly on my friend's lap and Paula had been trying to tell me that the jury leader wasn't reading from any pieces of paper and she and her sister had realised that he was going to be found guilty on all charges, but I was too upset to notice them.

I turned and Daniel and I shared an indescribable look. Clapping broke out from behind us and Paula turned to the people, some strangers, and told them not to clap. She said that we were better than that and she was right.

There were some brief legal representations from the Prosecution and the Defence. Fletcher was refused bail and taken into custody, led away by the contingent of uniformed Corrective Services officers to gaol where he would await his sentence, which would be handed down at Gosford District Court on March, the 11th, 2005.

Bernard and I both hugged Detective Peter Fox and then moved over to where Daniel was sitting, Luke's arms still around him. I remember looking at Luke who was sobbing and saying that he was crying more than his brother and Daniel just looked up at me and said "but Mum, I knew he was guilty."

26

Relief! Relief and hugging. Tears and more hugging of the police, the media, the sheriff and each other. Daniel's face was transformed as he smiled through his tears. We jostled about in the narrow passageway outside the courtroom for a few minutes and then were overcome with the need to tell the close family who weren't with us that day. Bernard went outside to ring Dominic and saw his father moving towards the steps of thc Courthouse. He sensed immediately there was news because of all the people outside on phones and hurried inside after Bernard told him the verdict. I saw him coming up the stairs and the look we exchanged was pure relief. I know we cried on each other's shoulders for quite a few minutes.

I stood in a quiet spot and tried to ring my sisters. After several attempts to dial with shaking fingers I managed connections but all I could sob out were the words "he's guilty of everything, all nine charges" and I asked them to contact their daughters, the much loved cousins.

Somehow we were back in the room and our legal team came in. They were thrilled with the verdict of course and we were very grateful for their dedication. I know they work to prosecute criminals every week but to us, it had been unfamiliar territory and we were very impressed.

The media waited outside and we did appreciate them for not being intrusive but they did want a comment from the victim or his family. Daniel said he couldn't speak and so I fossicked in my bag for a prepared statement that I had shown John earlier in the day, along with one that expressed our dismay if the verdict had been Not Guilty. Detective Peter Fox agreed to read my statement and walked outside with me.

He read "I would like to say that justice has been served today. The years of pain and suffering for the victims and their families can now be put behind. We hope that all of us can now move forward unhindered by these dreadful events. We commend the jury for their verdict."

He was too modest to read the rest of my statement and so I took it from him and read

"Detective Sergeant Peter Fox has shown my son and our family, commitment, compassion, diligence and integrity throughout this investigation and Trial and we thank him and commend him as well."

Detective Fox also said that he was very pleased with the result and called it a vindication of the courage of the two men who gave evidence during the trial.

He said "Their absolute courage in coming forward and being prepared to come along and say what they did before a packed court room took a hell of a lot of courage...I think today's result vindicates what they actually did.... I'm obviously very pleased with the result. I have worked closely with these families for two and a half years. I suppose in some ways, police do go a little bit through the ordeal and share some of the emotion with it...I personally feel the result vindicates the effort put in by these two families."

Later a media person asked would we be celebrating and I replied that the sentiment was relief not joy because a paedophile had just been convicted of abusing my son and there was nothing to celebrate in that.

We gathered in the room for the last time and I had a half hearted attempt to have a bite of the lunchtime sandwich and a mouthful of tea but I responded very readily to the suggestion that we all adjourn to the nearest pub. Once there, we took stock of the last few hours and debriefed I suppose. We welcomed the presence of Peter Fox and supporters as we reflected on the trial and started to remember that Christmas was less than three weeks away.

Workers finished for the day started to gather at the hotel and the sheer ordinariness of the day for other people amazed me. I thought that because our lives had been so dreadfully connected to the trauma of the past few weeks, the effect would have been visible to strangers but I was wrong. There we were gathering after years of major upset and the rest of the world didn't know and probably wouldn't have cared if they did. Such is the nature of our insular society.

The mobile phones were ringing and we took turns using them ourselves as we informed the extended family of the verdict. I noticed John on his phone over under a tree and then he gestured for Daniel to take it. John walked over to me and told me that Daniel was talking to the Bishop. It was one hour after the verdict.

Daniel spoke for a few minutes and I wondered how his conversation was going and became increasingly distracted the longer he talked. John said the bishop had expressed concern for all the family and praised our courageous son and we both wondered what the message would have been if the verdict had gone the other way. When Daniel walked over to us after talking with the Bishop, he was upset and also queried what would have been said if Fletcher had been found Not Guilty. I remember his father saying not to waste time thinking about it as there wouldn't have been a phone call at all.

This boy has struggled along without moral support from the very organisation that had helped mould his soul and psyche. Its agent and employee, the priest, had destroyed his belief in it as well as his innocence. A double loss was sustained by my boy who had yearned for some kind of faith mantle to protect him through the painful months that had just passed.

We were astounded then when he told us that the Bishop had told him to "keep his faith" and praised him "for having the courage to come forward and bring this terrible man to justice." No sorry words and that's what he had wanted to hear from the Bishop and of course Fletcher himself.

The media had plenty to write about and there was scope for many angles of commentary. The Bishop faced a very hostile community as people realised that a paedophile had worked in their midst while facing very serious charges of sexual assault. He admitted that he could have handled the James Fletcher controversy in a better manner, and publicly apologised for failing to stand down the convicted paedophile immediately after being told of the child sex allegations.

"It is easy to have 20-20 vision after the event," he said.

"In retrospect, the matter could have been handled better and we have learned that we have to respond more appropriately to these issues. To this end we are establishing a diocesan child protection unit to respond more professionally in future." he added.

Bishop Malone wrote to Daniel, John and me the next day. I guess by then he had had time to digest the news and reflect on the awful ramifications for the Church. He said in his letter to me,

"On behalf of the Diocese of Maitland-Newcastle, I apologise profoundly to you for the trauma, pain, and suffering you have experienced at the hands of Fr. Fletcher. There is no room in the priesthood for such a man: he will never return to ministry as a priest. The Police investigation and subsequent Trial have been very difficult for you. I can only imagine a fraction of the trauma you must have felt knowing that you would have to speak of these matters publicly. I applaud your courage and thank you for coming forward so that this criminal could be put away."

He offered further support in the way of counselling and a meeting with him if I so desired.

I am pleased the Bishop rang after the Trial and I did appreciate his letter and the spirit in which it was written. Not to have heard from the Church would have been the final thud in a long line of bitter disappointments, breach of trust and recriminations I had experienced because I had kept the faith of my parents and had tried to pass it on to my sons, my beloved sons.

Epilogue

Gosford Court March the 29th 2005

Prisoner James Patrick Fletcher was brought before the Court for sentencing. He looked dishevelled and was stooped, had long hair and unsteady gait.

We sat through another summary of the crimes. This time there was a representative of the Maitland- Newcastle Catholic Diocese to support us if necessary. Detective Fox spoke warily with her. Daniel did not attend. The Defence had talked about prospects for rehabilitation and the Crown immediately rebutted that request, saying that as Fletcher did not acknowledge his guilt, rehabilitation was not an issue at all. The program offered by Corrective Services to educate sex offenders and to endeavour to rehabilitate them was obviously viable for those criminals who admitted their crimes.

Distressingly, Ian Barker QC for Fletcher, argued that there were mitigating factors for the judge to consider when sentencing Fletcher. They were the public humiliation for the priest and the lack of victim impact statement from my son, meaning long term trauma may not be suffered. We were appalled as Daniel and his family had been told that such statements were not necessary.

Judge Armitage questioned Barker's argument saying that in evidence about the first time my son was molested by Fletcher, Daniel had said it "was excruciating and he'd never felt anything like it."

"He made it abundantly plain he was traumatised." Judge Armitage said.

After lengthy legal representations from both sides, the judge announced that the sentencing would take place at Sydney's District Court's Downing Centre on April the 11th, 2005

The Downing Centre, Sydney

Sydney District Court heard that in a "gross and inexcusable misuse of trust" James Patrick Fletcher had ingratiated himself with the boy and his family, had meals at their home and had lured him away at night for sex. Judge Graham Armitage said the now former Hunter parish priest continued to protest his innocence in the face of some of the most compelling evidence he had heard from a young victim. He said the victim had presented as a down-to-earth young man who was truthful. Fletcher showed no emotion as Judge Armitage sentenced him to serve a maximum of ten years in gaol. He would not be eligible for parole until the 4th of June, 2012, after which he would have served seven and a half years.

Judge Armitage said when sentencing Fletcher that he had taken into account the priest's age, health and the fact he had no previous convictions.

My media statement was "This man's assaults on our son were premeditated and evil, and for our family the sentence is lifelong. No amount of time in prison can restore the joy in faith that was embraced and has now been lost by the victim, his family and the wider Catholic communities of our extended family and friends."

An Appeal against the conviction was lodged.

Bishop Michael Malone released a statement on the afternoon of April 12 saying he accepted the sentence as the judgement of the court. He also said his primary consideration was the care extended to the victim."Victims of sexual abuse and their families must be supported by their parish and community and not be subjected to victimisation or damaging innuendo," he said.

"We must not let them be criticised or ostracised for coming forward. In fact, they should be thanked for bringing abuse into the open."

He also strongly urged victims of sexual abuse to contact the police.

He announced the establishment of a Diocesan Child Protection Unit to deal with issues of sexual abuse and to monitor and comply with child protection legislation. A healing component of the unit was to be included.

Well done Bishop Michael!

First attendance at the Court of Criminal Appeal

The Appeal was based on the legality of the original Trial Judge allowing the similarity and tendency evidence of Fletcher's other victim. More summations of the whole trial. No decision reached. Diocesan representative, Helen Keevers criticised for not outwardly supporting the priest and his friends. I appreciated her attendance.

Second attendance at the Court of Criminal Appeal.

Another summation. Fletcher's counsel had argued the Trial Judge had erred in law because he had admitted evidence from a former alleged victim of Fletcher that was prejudicial to the case. His defence counsel had also argued that the judge had erred when instructing the jury about the use of evidence to show that the priest had a tendency to commit the offences. Justice Carolyn Simpson and Justice Peter McClellan agreed the prejudicial effect of the evidence against Fletcher was substantially outweighed by the probative value. Court rejected appeal by 2 votes to 1. I tried to be relieved but heard murmurings of an action to seek leave to Appeal to the High Court of Australia.

January, 4th 2006 Helen Keevers, the Manager of the Diocesan Child Protection Unit rang our family to inform us that James Fletcher had suffered a severe stroke and was not expected to live.

James Patrick Fletcher died on 6th January, 2006. Funeral of Fletcher was held at Branxton Catholic Church on 13th January. Thirty-four Catholic priests attended. A quiet reflective lunch was held in Hamilton for victims and their families while the funeral was taking place. This was organised by the Manager of the Child Protection unit, Helen Keevers and was appreciated by us. No messages from any of the clergy for the victims and families. We also pained.

The Appeal to the High Court was announced by Father Des Harrigan who said it was his duty as executor of Fletcher's will. He also said he sought peace for everyone associated with the case.

10th March, 2006 The High Court of Australia

The High Court of Australia rejected an appeal application on behalf of paedophile priest James Fletcher. Chief Justice Murray Gleeson and Justice Ken Hayne, sitting in Sydney, dismissed a special leave application by Father Des Harrigan to appeal against the dead priest's conviction. Barrister Ian Barker QC, for Father Harrigan, said that much of the evidence in question related to "different acts of a different sort in different circumstances" to those which Fletcher was found guilty. Chief Justice Gleeson disagreed saying, "We are of the view that the evidence in question was correctly admitted in the particular circumstances of this case and we are not persuaded there has been any miscarriage of justice."

Detective Sergeant Peter Fox said in a media interview that he shared the victims' relief and was pleased the High Court decision would benefit other child abuse victims. He reiterated that the appeal application was not about whether Fletcher had abused children or not but rather it was based on a legal technicality about tendency evidence being admitted to Fletcher's District Court trial.

He said "This decision means that the highest court in the land accepts that it was correct for the District Court to have allowed evidence from a second altar boy whom Fletcher abused and that will flow on to other courts so that they too can accept similar tendency evidence."

Zimmerman House opened on September 4th, 2007 and is the new premises for the Diocesan Child Protection Unit, established in 2005. This is a specialized, diocesan wide unit working in the areas of child protection, professional conduct and healing. Unit manager, Helen Keevers stated that the victims and survivors of abuse will be supported and "walked with…forever how long it takes!"

In an interview with Newcastle Herald journalist, Joanne McCarthy, Bishop Michael Malone was described as "an outspoken advocate for victims of paedophilia." That was in July, 2008 and followed the Bishop's "lone stand as a senior cleric in calling for the Pope to apologise during World Youth Day." He also said that the abuse of Daniel brought the whole issue home to him.

"It was a case of here's a priest invited into the Feenan home, shown love and friendship, and he abused that friendship so badly," Malone said "…I'd have to say my level of empathy has altered considerably from being fairly defensive of the Church, to where my primary responsibility these days is to the victims, and not the Church."

That change in attitude after seven long years in our lives is welcome and gives some hope for closure to my campaign to firstly seek recognition and ownership by the Catholic Church of the crime of clergy sexual abuse and secondly, compassion and Christ's love for the victims.

Well done Daniel! Your courage is amazing! You sought and secured justice and by doing that you have ensured that the pursuit of justice for others to come will have a better chance of success because of the change in the law. In addition, we hope that the Catholic Church will acknowledge the pain of the victims and will walk with them on the journey to recovery, for however long it takes.

Postscript

In the last few years, there have been numerous police charges of sexual abuse of children by more than five priests in the Maitland Newcastle Catholic Diocese. In addition, there have also been many allegations about priests who are now deceased. It would appear that the prosecution of James Fletcher was not the end of matters at all and the floodgates are open as victims find the strength to come forward and tell what happened to them. Certainly, victims are treated with respect and compassion, as Bishop Michael Malone promised, but the numbers are many and the Catholic communities are dismayed. Particularly stressful is the knowledge that there appears to have been many cover-ups by the Church hierarchy as they sought to protect the good name of the Church.

On the 16th of September 2012, a public meeting at Newcastle, attended by over 500 concerned people, endorsed the request to the Premier of New South Wales to establish a Royal Commission into the Catholic Church's handling of child sexual abuse within the church.

On the 8th of November 2012, Detective Chief Inspector Peter Fox was interviewed on ABC TV's Lateline program. In his interview, he asserted that his investigations had been hampered by the Church and in fact he was removed from another clergy sexual abuse case he was working on. He then proceeded to talk about the brutal rape of a young boy and the callous behaviour of the priest after the event. That boy was my son, and the public outcry after Detective Chief Inspector Peter Fox's interview resulted in the Premier of New South Wales announcing a special commission of inquiry in response to these claims on the next day, the 9th of November.

Responses to this announcement were varied. Whilst victims and families welcomed the inquiry, there were many statements from them, including mine, reported in the media, saying that a Royal Commission was what was needed to restore trust and to effectively examine the Catholic Church's handling of clergy sexual abuse. Many asserted that an inquiry centred on the Hunter region was too narrow.

On the afternoon of the 12th of November, the Prime Minister of Australia, Julia Gillard, announced that a nationwide Royal Commission into the handling of child sexual abuse by religious and other institutions was to be held, the most comprehensive inquiry into institutional abuse of children in Australia's history.

Relief!

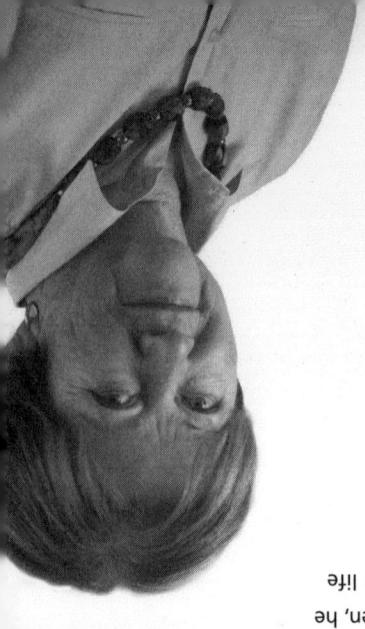

"This was my beloved son
in whom I was well pleased."

Patricia Feenan has been described as a strong and resilient woman. She has needed to be. Mother of four sons, a grandmother and teacher, she decided to write this story as a testament to her eldest son's courage in deciding to come forward and give evidence against a paedophile priest. Raised in a traditional Catholic family, she was totally unprepared for the shock of denial and ostracism by the church community. An advocate for victims of clergy sexual abuse, she is committed to making sure that her family's lonely experience will never be repeated.

Her mantra? "He picked the wrong woman's son to abuse!"

She also has another life where she enjoys travel, reading, gardening and quiet times in her home in the Hunter Valley.

Daniel Feenan has three beautiful children, he works very hard in his chosen career, his life isn't always easy but he is well and happy.